A CHURCH FOR ALL WEATHERS

A CHURCH FOR ALL WEATHERS

I shall tell in turn of the brave leaders of this whole race,
Its customs, its pursuits, its divisions and its battles.
(Virgil, Geo.IV.4-5)

A CHURCH FOR ALL WEATHERS

The 200-year history of
Donaghadee Methodist Church

KIT CHIVERS

Published by
Donaghadee Methodist Church

A CHURCH FOR ALL WEATHERS

First edition 2012

ISBN 978-0-9574087-0-8

Published by
Donaghadee Methodist Church,
2 Moat Street,
Donaghadee,
County Down
BT21 0DA

Copyright © 2012 Donaghadee Methodist Church
www.donaghadeemethodist.com

COVER PICTURE

The cover shows a baptism in the sea off Ballyvester,
County Down, in May 2011 *(Photo: Norma Best)*

PREFACE

Preface

This book was written to mark the 200th anniversary of the founding of Donaghadee Methodist Church, which was opened in May 1813.

It is a history in two parts, a century each. That happened by accident, as I was called away for most of a year after writing the first part and had to start afresh on the second hundred years.

There is a point in keeping the two halves separate. Writing ancient history is different from writing history which comes into the time people can remember. For the first hundred years there were only scraps of information to go on and one had to treasure every fragment. As the history gets closer to the present day the volume of material grows and the task is one of selecting what to report.

When writing Part Two I was able to draw on the personal memories of some of the older members of the congregation. An open meeting was held in the church in June 2011 to share recollections, some going as far back as the 1930s, and many of the 1940s, and members brought along old photographs, some of which are reproduced here. I am indebted to Maureen Bell, Elizabeth Bird, Billy Fergie and Dorothy Mills, who with Ken Halliday formed a panel to lead that discussion. It was to be the last occasion on which the Harbour Lights (p.109) performed.

Donaghadee Methodist is just one church in a small town in a corner of Northern Ireland. It is not a model church or an exceptional church, and its history is not, for the most part, dramatic. But this book testifies to the generations of faithful people who have worked so hard to keep the church going in good times and in less good, preaching the Word, caring for one another and for the community and generously supporting the worldwide work of the Church.

It is dedicated to those individuals, some of them named in the book but many more omitted, the full extent of whose service is known only to God.

KC   Donaghadee, 2012

Acknowledgements

Donaghadee Methodist Church acknowledges the generous help provided by the Wesley Historical Society, and in particular by its Archivist, the Rev Robin Roddie. It is also right to mention here that this work owes a great debt to local Donaghadee historian Mr Harry Allen, whose book is a constant source. Any errors are wholly the fault of the author, who would be glad to receive corrections and additions to the text.

Contents

Part One, 1813-1912

Page number

Chapter 1: The setting

Introduction	12
The town of Donaghadee	13
The port of Donaghadee	14
The political situation in 1813	18

Chapter 2: The advent of Methodism

John Wesley	26
Origins of the Society in Donaghadee	28
The first chapel in Donaghadee, 1813	33
Henrietta Gayer	34

Chapter 3: Building

Building the Chapel	37
Mary Smith	43
Relations with the Established Church	50
Methodism and Presbyterianism	55

Chapter 4: Re-building

The progress of Methodism	58
The first and second manses, 1822 and 1836	59
The great famine, 1845-51	64
The school, 1846, and rebuilding the church	66

Chapter 5: The spirit of the age

The Revival of 1859	68
The start of the modern era, the 1860s	69
Temperance	71
Music	73
Church life in the 1870s and 1880s	74

Chapter 6: The end of the era

Home Rule	78
The third manse, 1893, and reshaping the church	80
The spirit of Methodism	88
Conclusion	90

Appendices to Part One

1.	Extracts from the diary of Mrs Mary Smith	92
2.	Extracts from the Narrative of the Rev Dr Matthew Lanktree	95
3.	Notes on the Baptismal Register, 1825-1849	100
4.	Ministers at Donaghadee, year by year	104

CONTENTS

Part Two, 1913-2012

Chapter 7: The First War

Donaghadee in 1913	110
- Home Rule	112
Rev Henry McConnell (1912-1915)	113
- The church schools in 1913	115
Rev Robert Maxwell (1915-1919)	117

Chapter 8: The inter-war years

Rev Robert Teasey (1919-1923)	120
Rev William McVitty (1923-1926)	123
Rev William E Maguire (1926-1928)	125
Rev William Bryans (1928-1930)	125
Rev Charles Wilson (1930-1934)	126
- Childhaven and the Belfast City Mission	128
Rev Francis Scott Maguire (1934-1939)	129
- The Church Schools in the 1930s	131

Chapter 9: War and recovery

Rev Robert McDonagh (1939-1944)	133
- The Second World War	134
Rev Samuel McIntyre (1944-1946)	137
Rev Samuel Baxter (1947-1952)	139
- The second church organ	141

Chapter 10: Salad days

Rev Samuel Crawford (1952-1955)	145
Rev Thomas Kyle (1955-1960)	152

Rev Robert Good (1960-1965)   157

Chapter 11: The climate changes

Rev Frank Bolster (1965-1973)   160
   - The Troubles   165
Rev Wesley Gray (1973-1981)   168
   - The Great Fire   170
Rev Wilfred Agnew (1981-1987)   173
Rev George Campbell (1988-1993)   175
   - Youth work in Donaghadee   180
Rev David Houston (1993-1994)   182

Chapter 12: The once and future church

Rev Lee Glenny (1994-2001)   183
Rev Robert Russell (2001-2009)   187
Rev Ruth Craig (2009 - current date)
   - and the present state of the church   195

Appendices to Part Two

1. The Church Council and other officers   200
2. Ministers at Donaghadee 1913-2012   202
3. Photographs of church organisations   204

Postscript   209
Bibliography   211
Index   213

PART ONE

Part One:
The first hundred years
1813-1912

Mary Carey

A plaque at the front of the church reads:

"Converted in 1791, she became the pioneer of Sunday School work in this area. She gradually overcame much opposition and established a preaching house in a barn at her home, for the proclamation of the gospel. She lived to see the erection of the Methodist Church in Donaghadee, and on 28 March 1868, aged 96 years, she passed home to be with God and her Saviour, Jesus Christ. She is regarded in the town as the Mother of Methodism, and her remains lie in the Parish Church yard."

Chapter 1
The setting

Introduction

The Methodist Church opened its first chapel in Donaghadee in 1813. There had been a Methodist society in Donaghadee from around 1790. At first its members travelled into Newtownards or Belfast to worship, then they began to conduct their own services, first in a disused corn-kiln close to the site of the present church and later, as their numbers increased, in a barn belonging to the father of Mary Carey, one of the founding members. Then in 1812 a well-to-do lady called Mary Smith, who was related to the landowner of Donaghadee, Daniel Delacherois, obtained from him a lease of the current church site and organised a subscription to build a permanent chapel there. The original church was rebuilt in 1849, refurbished in 1882 and then substantially remodelled in 1909.

More of that in due course. But first, what was Donaghadee like in 1813? What sort of town was it? What was going on there, and what were the influences that led to the establishment of a Methodist chapel?

THE SETTING

The town of Donaghadee

We are fortunate to be able to draw on the excellent history of Donaghadee by local historian Harry Allen[1]. In 1813 Donaghadee was a town of about 2000 people, with perhaps another 1000 living in the countryside around it but still in the parish of Donaghadee. At that stage it was bigger than Bangor, which did not overtake it in size until 1850. A survey in 1837 showed that there were 650 houses in the town, of which 430 were single storey cottages. We may guess that there were rather fewer than that in 1813, and the proportion that were single storey would have been greater. The majority of houses were roofed with slates from Ballygrainey, but about a quarter were still thatched.

The town extended from East Street (then known as Bullock Row, because it was the way down which cattle were driven to the port) to Manor Street, then known as Back Street. Moat Street was called Mound Street and Millisle Road was called Barrack Hill. New Street had only recently, in 1780, been cut through from the High Street to Shore Street, or Sandy Row. There was as yet no residential development out along the Warren Road. To the south of the harbour, before the railway was built, the sea came further inland between the harbour and the quarry (now the marina) to form Salt Pan Bay, where there was a business of boiling seawater in iron pans to make salt.

---

[1] *Donaghadee, an illustrated history,* published by The White Row Press, 2006

All the streets were rough clay and stones, with only a few areas paved with setts. There was no main drainage, and sanitation would have been primitive. The water supply was taken from a variety of hand pumps reaching down into wells, and it was no doubt pollution of one or more of those wells that led to the serious outbreak of cholera in 1832.

Despite that, the surveyors in 1837 commented condescendingly on "a greater degree of cleanliness than is usual in Ireland" and noted that the town needed only three policemen because "the people were sober and peaceable and not much given to amusement". They noted that no illegal distillation was carried on, but that may have been because it was rendered unnecessary by the amount of smuggling that went on, especially through the unpoliced Copeland Islands.

But if Donaghadee was "peaceable" by 1837, it had certainly not been so forty years earlier. We shall come to the political situation presently, but first it is important to understand the economics of the town, and why it was the town it was.

The port of Donaghadee

In 1813 Donaghadee was an important seaport. It was a main passenger terminal not just for the North of Ireland but for Ireland as a whole. In those days of small sailing ships many passengers – and most importantly the Royal Mail - preferred to make the 72-hour journey from London to Dublin via Donaghadee, with its short sea crossing from Portpatrick, rather than taking their chances on crossing the Irish Sea from

THE SETTING

Holyhead to Dublin, where the winds could cause unpredictable delays and the sea could be uncomfortably rough. We are told that of the four boats employed on the mail run it was a requirement that one should at all times be available in Donaghadee and one in Portpatrick, ready to carry the mail across as soon as a mail coach arrived from London or Dublin.

A road atlas of Ireland published in 1777 showed the road from Dublin to Donaghadee via Newry on its first two pages: it was in effect the Irish M1 or N1 of its day. Belfast was by then beginning to become significant as a commercial port, but Donaghadee was preferred by passengers up till about 1840, when larger, faster steamships, which could not use Donaghadee's harbour, began to open up alternative routes[2].

In 1813 the traffic through Donaghadee was at its peak, with around 20,000 passengers and 30,000 cattle passing through each year. The present harbour was not constructed until 1825, but a new harbour had been built in 1774 with a pier starting at right angles from the foot of the current pier and curving out half way across the current harbour. That was big enough for the small craft of that day, which were designed to be beached at low tide. The passage to Portpatrick was served by 50-ton cutters, sailing ships with a single mast carrying the usual cutter rig of gaff, jib and staysail but also square-rigged with course,

---

[2] Belfast did not have deep water access to the sea until the Victoria Channel was dredged in 1840, though paddle steamers were able to make their way across the sand bars at high tide before then. The Rev Matthew Lanktree, who appears later in this history, was able to take a steamer from Belfast to Glasgow in 1819.

topsail and topgallant, giving them considerable speed in a good wind. In the early 1800's there were nearly 500 sailings a year from Donaghadee, carrying more than 25,000 tons of freight, mainly cattle and grain. In addition there would have been fishing smacks in the harbour, where catches of herring were landed to be processed.

It was therefore a prosperous, as well as a strategically important port. There were a number of wealthy people living in Donaghadee, not just the Delacherois family but substantial business people and officials connected with the port. There was actually something of a social scene. The Rev Hill records (with disapproval) that:

> "Many wealthy families then resided in Donaghadee, and what was called fashionable life was the rule. Feasting, dancing and gaming: these were eagerly pursued as innocent amusements and needful recreation."[3]

Between 1821 and 1825 the present harbour was built, designed to take the new paddle steamers. But the advent of steam also marked the beginning of a relative decline, with traffic to Dublin going direct from Liverpool or Holyhead and with Belfast's own harbour being dredged to take the new steamships. For a time the decline was only relative, because the volume of traffic was increasing on all routes. Donaghadee contuned to be a busy port until, by the middle of the century, the ferry boats in use became too big even for Donaghadee's new harbour and

---

[3] The Rev John Hill, who published memorials of Mrs Smith and Miss Smith in 1858.

THE SETTING

Donaghadee had to re-invent itself as a seaside holiday and residential town instead of a commercial port.

Donaghadee harbour in the second half of the C 19th

In 1813 trade was flourishing. The second half of the 18th century had been a period of rising prosperity in this part of Ireland, and the founding of the Methodist Chapel co-incided with an additional economic boom created by the Napoleonic War. While the war was being waged the Army and Navy needed provisions of all kinds - wood, metal and textiles - and at the same time high food prices benefited farmers everywhere. The money that made possible the building of the chapel in 1812 – 1813 was most likely generated by that upsurge of trade, soon though it was to come to an end[4]. Shore Street and First Presbyterian Churches were likewise built in the early 1820s.

---

[4] The ending of the Napoleonic wars in 1815 led to a sharp recession in the years that followed. The Irish Methodist Conference in 1820 reported to the British Conference a financial deficit of £2000 in terms which sound uncannily contemporary:

The political situation in 1813

The increasing prosperity of the middle class in 18th century Ireland was accompanied by political unrest, which affected Donaghadee deeply at the turn of the century. Most of the island of Ireland was farmed by Catholics, who were not allowed to own land but rented their farms from Anglican landlords and had to pay tithes to the Anglican church. Ireland had its own Parliament in Dublin, but Catholics were excluded from it and from all public offices. The increasing wealth and education of some Catholics, in the cities and in the countryside, did not sit easily with a continued denial of political rights. And among the educated classes there was a growing interest in the early history of Ireland and a sense of its national status, which played into the movement for Home Rule.

In 1782 there had been a reform of the Dublin Parliament which purported to give more rights to Catholics, but there was little substance to the reforms. Catholics were not relieved of the discrimination against them[5]. So while some Catholics backed the new Parliament, others lost patience and started to think increasingly in terms of independence from Britain,

---

"The state of Ireland is at present deplorable. The decline of commerce, depression of trade, want of employment and latterly the sudden deterioration of the Banks in our Southern Districts, have reduced the country to a state of almost unparalleled distress."

[5] The Penal Laws, under which Catholics were not only excluded from public employment but were denied education and restricted in where they were allowed to live, were not repealed until 1793. Catholic emancipation had to wait till 1829.

THE SETTING

inspired by the independence recently achieved (1776) by the American colonies.

In 1789 the French stormed the Bastille and a wave of revolutionary fervour swept over Europe. Presbyterians in Ireland, like their colleagues in the Church of Scotland, had been supporters of the Americans in their War of Independence a few years earlier, and many of them now felt their sympathies lying with the French revolutionaries. And so it was that many Catholics and Presbyterians found themselves in agreement about the case for independence from Britain.

Wolfe Tone was one of the three founders of the Society of the United Irishmen in 1791. It started as a constitutional party, based in Belfast, but when Britain declared war on France in 1793 it became a secret society whose aims were revolutionary. By 1797 it had 280,000 members, North and South but particularly in the North. When the police raided its headquarters in Belfast in that year they discovered among its secret papers the Donaghadee Resolutions, a revolutionary manifesto based on the American Declaration of Independence[6]. The Resolutions called for the right of the

---

[6] The leading Methodist Dr Coke, who visited Donaghadee in March 1797, observed intense political activity in the town. He wrote that "The whole province is in violent agitation and seems to be preparing itself for some astonishing blow." (Crookshank, Vol 1, p.119). The fact that they were called the *Donaghadee Resolutions* suggests that at least one of their authors came from Donaghadee. It is not impossible that one or two people from Donaghadee were among the set of Irish, American and English radicals (including Thomas Paine and Mary Wollstonecraft) who gathered in White's Hotel in Paris in the early years after the French Revolution.

people to self-determination, the abolition of tithes[7] and the establishment of a Revolutionary Committee on the lines of the French Revolutionary Government.

In the North, the United Irishmen were strongest to the East of the Bann. East of the Bann many of the wealthier Presbyterians were involved in manfacturing and commerce rather than in agriculture, so they were not so directly in competition with Catholics. West of the Bann, Protestant farmers were more suspicious of their Catholic neighbours and less willing to make common cause with them. There was continuing violence between groups like the Protestant Peep o' Day Boys and the Catholic Defenders, which the authorities found it useful to foment because it helped to undermine the United Irishmen.

It was in the West that Loyalism flourished and the Orange Order was founded, while in the East, in places like Donaghadee, the local Presbyterians included many United Irishmen with revolutionary sympathies willing to ally with Catholic nationalists. In fact several of the leaders of the United Irishmen in this part of the island were Presbyterian clergymen. Anglicans (Wolfe Tone being an exception) tended to be loyal to the British Crown, and among Protestants Methodists distinguished themselves from their Presbyterian neighbours by

---

[7] It was the sudden re-imposition or re-enforcement of tithes in the Ards in 1792 that was one of the triggers for the the growth of disaffection in that area.

THE SETTING

their loyalty to the Crown[8]. A friend wrote to Matthew Lanktree from Coleraine:

> "The Methodists in this town were much against taking up arms, until imperative necessity demanded it; but so soon as that appeared, we did not wait for asking, but were determined to die before we would desert our good king in time of trouble."

The Rev Randall Phillips[9] records that:

> "The well-known attachment of the Methodist people to the Constitution preserved them from molestation on the part of the military, but it also exposed them to the persecution of the rebels; though in general their preachers were permitted to travel wherever they liked and laboured safely in the disturbed districts."

Matthew Lanktree confirms that in his *Narrative*:

> "Notwithstanding the indications of rebellion which marked the commencement of 1798 and increased as it advanced, notwithstanding assassinations, fearful apprehensions and military movements, we were suffered

---

[8] John Wesley had always been loyal to King George, and wrote influential pamphlets criticising the demands of the American colonies for independence. They were to cost him his control of the Methodist Church in America when independence was declared. Wesley did not believe in democracy.

[9] In *Irish Methodism*, 1897.

to labour on, to travel unmolested and preach the word of life in all our regular places."

Wolfe Tone started to negotiate with the French in 1794, with a view to gaining French support for an uprising in Ireland. These were very difficult days for Britain, which was no match for the French on land and was only saved from invasion by its Navy. However, the main French attempt on Ireland came to grief in storms off Bantry Bay in 1796, and although there were a few further attempts at invasion in the following years they were on a smaller scale (Napoleon had by now turned the main focus of his attention to the East[10]) and the British were able to repel them with little difficulty.

However, the authorities discovered in 1796 that the main threat was not the French, but the United Irishmen. They imposed martial law, which led to beatings and other injustices and further inflamed the population. That resulted in the open rebellion of 1798, in which Donaghadee played a major part. The port and the barracks[11] were held by the United Irishmen for nearly a week, but they were eventually defeated in battles at Saintfield, Portaferry, Newtownards and, decisively, at

---

[10] In his exile on St Helena he is said to have regretted, with hindsight, that he did not throw his weight behind the Irish rebellion instead of opting for his ill-fated expedition to Egypt. But for that, the Battle of the Nile might have been fought off the Copeland Islands.

[11] Those same barracks were purchased for the second Methodist Manse (*Christian Advocate,* 26 Aug 1892), but did not prove satisfactory for that purpose and were very soon replaced by 'Wesley Lodge', built on the same site in 1836.

THE SETTING

Ballynahinch. Wolfe Tone was captured later that year, sentenced to death and died of a self inflicted injury in prison. 30,000 Irishmen died that year, which gives an idea of the scale of the rebellion. It is also indicative of the extent to which it was a civil war between opposing factions in Ireland, not just a war between rebels and the British Crown[12].

As Loyalists, Methodists played an active role in putting down the rebellion. They could not join the local Yeomanry (the equivalent of the Territorial Army) because they drilled on a Sunday, but they fought alongside them. Randall Phillips records this incident at Monasteravan, Co. Kildare, which was besieged by rebels in 1798. It features, incidentally, the Rev Adam Averell, whom we shall encounter later as a founding Trustee of Donaghadee Methodist Church:

> "Early next morning, under cover of a dense fog, the rebels advanced on the town. The Rev Adam Averell, who was staying there, engaged in prayer on behalf of the defenders, and when the first detachment of the besiegers neared the bridge the gallant body of Methodists poured so heavy a fusillade upon them ... that they were driven back with heavy loss."

---

[12] The cruelty is illustrated by what happened in Wexford, as recorded in Lanktree's *Narrative*. Prisoners taken by the rebels were led out one by one to be piked before being thrown into the river, until a Catholic priest put a stop to the barbarity. The one prisoner who survived happened to be a Methodist. That is one of several friendly mentions of Catholic priests in Lanktree's *Narrative*. He showed himself remarkably ecumenical in his approach.

Was there ever a Methodist militia anywhere but in Ireland?

After the rebellion had been put down there was still widespread disaffection, and Ireland remained strategically a weak link so far as the British Government was concerned. But instead of making concessions to conciliate those who had sympathised with the rebels, London responded by passing the 1800 Act of Union, abolishing the Dublin Parliament and giving the Irish constituencies, still un-reformed and undemocratic, seats at Westminster instead. It was not until 1829 that Catholic emancipation was granted in Ireland, and all through the 19th century Ireland was governed on a very tight rein from London. Civil liberties, such as *habeas corpus,* were suspended for most of the first half of the century.

The troubles of 1798 had a direct impact on Donaghadee. The port was closed for two years, either as a punishment or on security grounds, and when it was re-opened it was initially subject to tight security, with passports being required for all passengers. The volume of trade dipped sharply for a few years. To make matters worse, the rebellion was followed by a failure of the harvest in 1799, and widespread starvation in 1800.

That was the political context in which Daniel Delacherois granted a site for the building of a Methodist chapel[13]. Why would he do that?

---

[13] By contrast Colonel Ward, who owned Bangor, resisted the building of a Methodist chapel there until 1820.

THE SETTING

As we shall see, there were personal reasons as well as political ones, but the political reality was that the population of Donaghadee was overwhemingly non-conformist, with only perhaps the top five per cent of society safely in the Anglican Church, and the rebellion of 1798 was very recent. No doubt it suited him and the other people of means who contributed to Mary Smith's subscription to have these dissenters in a loyal, Establishment-oriented church rather than exposed to the Whiggery, Home Rulery and downright Republicanism that were prevalent in the Presbyterian Church[14].

We shall look further at the relationship between the Anglican and Methodist Churches in this period presently, but first we need to backtrack fifty years to the origins of Methodism in Ireland.

---

[14] D L Cooney says that "Of the four main churches in Ireland, only the Methodists could be said to be consistently on the side of the Government". Methodist Societies were conservative and religious, and had no sympathy for French revolutionary ideas. An anonymous commentator in 1814 argued that the Methodists ought to get a financial subvention from the State in recognition of their loyalty. He was indignant that they had received nothing, whereas the disloyal Dissenters had been rewarded, and even the Catholics had been appeased by the grant of the seminary at Maynooth.

Chapter 2
The advent of Methodism

John Wesley

John Wesley made no less than 21 visits to Ireland. He was a good sailor, and he braved the direct crossing to Dublin on most of those occasions, but he also made a number of crossings via Donaghadee. The following are extracts from his *Journal*:

> May 1, 1765: John Wesley's journey from Portpatrick
>
> "The wind was quite fair, so as soon as the tide served I went on board. It seemed strange to cross the sea in an open boat, especially when the waves ran high. I was a little sick until I fell asleep. In 5½ hours we reached Donaghadee: but my mare could not land until five hours later so that I did not reach Newtownards until half past eight."[15]

Crookshank adds that he spent a day there "endeavouring to lift up the hands of a poor, scattered, dejected people"[16].

---

[15] According to a family tradition, on this occasion Wesley stayed at the house in Newtownards belonging to an ancestor of one of the current church members, Mr Dermot Thompson.

[16] Crookshank Vol 1, p.182

THE ADVENT OF METHODISM

March 29th, 1767:

"The packet boat was ready in the morning but waited for the mail, hour after hour, until half past three in the afternoon. Thereby we avoided a violent storm and had only what they called a fresh breeze: however this breeze drove us to Donaghadee (thirty miles) in about three hours."

29th July, 1767: Journey from Newry

"I headed on to Donaghadee but found all the packet boats on the other side. So I agreed with the captain of a small vessel and went on board at 2 o'clock, but it was so late when we landed (after a passage of five hours) that we could only reach Stranraer that night." (On this visit he spent 4 months in Ireland).

The first Methodist Society in Ireland was formed in Dublin in 1747. In 1752 Wesley appointed Joseph Cownley to work in the North of Ireland, together with Robert Swindells and John Edwards. The Newry Circuit began in 1765, and included the North East of Ireland. The Belfast Circuit first appeared in the Minutes of Conference in 1780: it took in North Down and the Ards, which were at first served only by visiting preachers. We are told[17] that in 1786 the Wesleyan Ministers Howe and Grace from Belfast preached in Donaghadee. Ulster was the last province in which Methodism made headway, but by 1800 the

---

[17] Hill, p6

number of Methodists in Ulster was two thirds of the total for Ireland. The Ards Mission (to which Comber was added in 1820) was begun in 1818 with the appointment of the Rev Matthew Lanktree; and in 1820 a separate Donaghadee and Newtownards Circuit was constituted. Donaghadee was to become an independent Circuit in 1869.

Origins of the Society in Donaghadee

In 1959 the Rev Thomas Kyle, then Minister at Donaghadee Methodist Church, compiled a short history of the church to celebrate the fiftieth anniversary of the rebuilding in 1909. In it he describes the founding of the chapel as follows, drawing on Crookshank's *History*[18]:

> "Around the year 1790 there were a few Methodists in Donaghadee. As a result of the visits of some preachers[19] from Belfast a young woman named Mary Carey was led to trust Jesus as her Saviour, and as Crookshank in his *History of Methodism* says: "No sooner did she realise a conscious sense of sins forgiven, than she joined the little band of Methodists. This step brought the censure of her neighbours, who looked upon the Society as apostates

---

[18] Crookshank's *History of the Methodist Church in Ireland*, published in 1885, is the main source of information about the early history of the church in Donaghadee.

[19] Crookshank (Vol 2, p.46) says that the Methodist community in Donaghadee at this time comprised "a few people in exceedingly humble cicumstances". They had been visited by preachers from Belfast, but at this time those preachers had, for whatever reason, ceased to visit.

from the faith of their fathers; and even her parents were influenced by the common prejudice and opposed her. However, by patient continuance in well-doing, she overcame much opposition and was permitted to act according to her convictions. Feeling her need for the social means of grace, she was accustomed to go four [Irish] miles to attend Society meetings, and even walked fourteen [to Belfast] to be present at Love-feasts[20]. Not satisfied, however, that the town should be neglected, she went on foot to Belfast, and with tears besought the preachers to return; and they consented. The place of meeting at first was a corn-kiln[21]; but Mary so influenced her parents that they invited the servants of God to their house, and the barn[22] was fitted up for their services. The Word preached was accompanied by Power from on High, several were converted, and the work prospered. Mary now had many companions with whom she had Christian fellowship, and by whom she was much beloved.

---

[20] Love feasts were named after the fellowship meals of the Early Church. A biscuit was eaten and water was passed round in a 'loving cup'. As it reached each person they were invited to testify about their religious experience since the last meeting. Love feasts often ended Circuit Quarterly Meetings in the C 19th.

[21] The corn-kiln would have been a small barn in which grain could be dried for storage. A fire would be lit outside the barn, and warm air would be drawn in to pass under the grain, which would be piled on a timber platform inside. It is believed that this corn-kiln was near the entrance to what is now the church car park, to the left of the entrance coming in.

[22] The barn is said by Rev R M Morrison (*Christian Advocate,* 10 Dec 1902) to have been located just off the High Street, on the West side.

> Persevering in work for Christ, she collected a number of neglected children in the barn each Lord's Day and taught them the Scriptures. This was the first Sunday School in that locality[23]."

An article by W. J. Thompson in the Irish Christian Advocate in December 1932 also describes the origins of Methodism in Donaghadee, as follows:

> "When Methodist preachers first visited Donaghadee, the open streets were their pulpits for holding forth the Word of Life. A few people in humble circumstances, but of deep and consistent piety, formed the first Society. For a long time it had no place of meeting but a disused corn-kiln. A gifted young lady called Mary Carey got converted, joined the little Society and obtained permission from her father to use his barn for their meetings. She laboured faithfully to bring sinners to repentance. It is said that in her old age it was her custom to feel the knees of the newly-appointed preachers to see if they were men of much prayer.

---

[23] Sunday schools were just taking off in this period. Robert Raikes of Gloucester is credited with opening the first Sunday School in 1780, though there had been occasional examples of such schools in dissenting chuches before then. As a journalist he was able to publicise the Sooty Alley project, and it was as a result of his writing that the Sunday School movement spread rapidly. It was viewed with profound suspicion by the Established Church and other conservatives: Members even spoke against it in Parliament, denouncing it as a dangerous sort of radicalism. This opposition is reflected in the text of the plaque to Mary Carey reproduced on page 11. Adults as well as children often attended the early schools.

"Shortly after Mary Carey's appearance, another talented lady, Miss Smith, cast in her lot with the Society. These winsome and determined ladies often preached in the streets of the town, even during the Rebellion of 1798. Other ladies of refinement and education, as well as more illiterate folk, joined themselves to the Methodists."

Mary Carey, a founding member of the Methodist Society in Donaghadee, "felt the knees of new preachers to see if they were men of much prayer"

Interestingly, however, Miss Jane McCutcheon of Rostrevor, granddaughter of a former Minister of Donaghadee, replied to the article, commenting as follows about Mary Carey[24]:

---

[24] *Christian Advocate,* 8th January 1933

"The traditions about her which I heard from my Mother (who knew her about 1842) are not quite the same as those in your article. As far as I can now tell, my Mother thought Miss Smith had a friend, another lady, who probably lived with her, and Mary Carey was their confidential maid or housekeeper. I do not think she was by birth or education what is usually called a "lady" – though she certainly was a saint, and a woman of ability. I believe it was Miss Smith and her friend (whose name I do not know[25]) who bought the old manse[26] and gave it to the Society, with the condition that Mary Carey should have two rooms in it while she lived. When my grandfather was stationed there first she lived in the manse, having the two rooms which could be shut off from the rest of the house, but she had the junior Minister[27] in one of them as a sort of lodger, and she looked after him."

---

[25] It was in fact her younger sister Anne, the second Miss Smith.

[26] This refers to the manse Mrs Smith built for the church in 1836.

[27] Junior Ministers were those who had not yet completed 10 years in the Ministry. They were not entitled to a manse and were paid only about 60 per cent of a Senior Minister's stipend. For that reason they were not allowed to marry without permission, as the stipend was not enough to support a wife. They did not attend Conference. The distinction only finally disappeared in the 1970s.

THE ADVENT OF METHODISM

The first chapel in Donaghadee, 1813

Mary Carey may have been the backbone of the Society in Donaghadee, but the driving force behind the building of a chapel was Mary Smith. Kyle writes:

> "Having occasion to visit Lisburn, she called on Mrs Gayer of Derriaghy, who enquired how the work of God prospered in the town; and being informed that the Society was poor and their place of worship a little barn, gave her five guineas[28], saying, "Take this, and commence to build a house for the worship of God." Other friends thus encouraged added their contributions, and on her return home Mrs Smith had thirty guineas.
>
> "Mr Steele, the Superintendent of the Circuit, undertook to collect the remainder of the needed funds, and thus the first Methodist Chapel was erected in Donaghadee. After a few years, Mrs Smith had a house built beside the chapel for a preacher's residence, at her own expense[29]."

---

[28] It is extremely hard to translate money of 1813 into money today, and there is no one correct way of doing it, since the prices of things do not increase uniformly. But if £12 to 15 was a labourer's wage for a year in Ireland at that time we could think of five guineas equating to more than £5,000 in local purchasing power (though it would not have bought a ball-gown for a lady in London); so Mrs Smith's collection produced roughly £30,000 in today's money, or maybe about a quarter of what they would have needed.

[29] This manse dated from around 1822 and served until 1836, when Miss Smith bought the site of the old military barracks on Millisle Road for £71 and built a new

Mrs Gayer of Derriaghy

Donaghadee's first benefactress, Mrs Gayer, provides a direct link back to John Wesley.

Henrietta Gayer, daughter of Mr Valentine Jones of Lisburn, was an early convert to Methodism and "an intimate friend" of Mr Wesley, who had several such female friends and admirers, often but not always in the higher levels of society. Beautiful, we are told, a charming singer and fond of dancing, she was to give up such diversions and devote herself to good works. She became the *doyenne* of the Methodist Society in Lisburn, helping to fund their first small chapel in 1770 and its grander replacement in 1788.

She inherited a considerable fortune in her own name when her husband died, but lived very simply and gave all the money away, carefully and prayerfully, so that she died in 1814 with nothing remaining. The five guineas she donated in 1812 was probably, therefore, a significant part of what she had left at that time.

Crookshank says that her husband Edward, whom she married in 1758, was Clerk to the Irish House of Lords, but that seems to be an error: it was Edward's brother William who held that office. According to Robert Haire, in *Wesley's one and twenty visits*

---

manse on its site. Kyle is following Crookshank, who is following Lanktree's *Narrative* at this point.

to Ireland, in 1773, when Wesley was 70 and on his fourteenth visit to Ireland:

> "Mrs Gayer heard Wesley preach, and at the close of the service was introduced to him. On obtaining her address, Wesley said he would visit her. Mrs Gayer, knowing that her husband Edward had no love for Methodism, and fearing a cold reception for Wesley, made it, along with her daughter [the 13-year old Mary, who had been with her at the preaching] a matter of earnest prayer during the greater part of the night. Next morning Wesley walked to Derryaghy, and on the avenue leading to the residence met a gentleman of whom he inquired if Mrs Gayer lived there. The gentleman replied, "Yes, she is my wife". Mr Gayer, not knowing the stranger, entered into conversation, and was so impressed with Wesley's culture and gentlemanly deportment that he invited him for dinner, and thus were the earnest prayers of the two ladies answered. Afterwards, Mr Gayer set aside a room in the house, and it was known as "The Prophet's Chamber".

Wesley was to use that room on future visits. On his next visit in 1775, at the age of 72, he fell seriously ill, so much so that he was unconscious or delirious for two or three days, and at times it was hard to detect a pulse. He was nursed through that illness by Henrietta and her (by then 16-year old) daughter Mary, with whom he was also greatly taken. Wesley, who knew his Shakespeare, wrote that as he saw Mary on one side of the bed, looking at her mother on the other, "Only these words ran in my mind: 'She sat like Patience on a monument, Smiling at grief'."

Mary Gayer became, according to William Smith, writing in 1830, "the pious and venerable Mrs Wolfenden of Dublin", whose son and daughter were both active in the Church. Wesley spent a couple of weeks convalescing at Derriaghy, and visited again in 1778 and 1789. The Wolfendens were friends of the Gayers. Wesley planted two trees on their Chrome Hill estate in 1787, which were designed to grow together and intertwine to symbolise the future reunion of Anglicanism and Methodism. A young relative of the Gayers called William Reeves was to become Bishop of Down, Connor and Dromore, so the Gayers must have remained an Establishment family on the male side, despite Henrietta's and Mary's conversion to Methodism.

Chapter 3
Building

Building the Chapel

Mrs Smith's thirty guineas was a valuable start to the fund-raising, but money was evidently very tight. As a result the physical work of building the chapel, as well as the task of raising most of the funds, seems largely to have fallen on the Superintendent, the Rev Samuel Steele[30], as noted in this memoir written by the Rev Matthew Lanktree and published in 1836:

> "The Wesleyan Society in Donaghadee had only a feeble commencement, but after a few years of humble effort, the Word of Truth struck deep root into a few hearts, where, cherished by faith and prayer and guarded by watchfulness it brought forth the fruits of righteousness, to the praise and glory of God. Their first place of worship was a small barn belonging to Antony Carey. Mary his daughter (now a Mother in Israel) by her faithful and affectionate regard to what she believed was the cause of God, greatly promoted the interests of the Society. After some time of patient continuance in well doing she was joined by Miss Smith, both of them being influenced by the same spirit were

---

[30] Steele was a significant figure in Methodism at the time. He was an able writer in defence of Methodism against its critics, and was one of the first to administer communion to his congregation in Armagh in 1815.

enabled to extend a happy influence around them over the different grades of society[31].

"Mr Steele built their Chapel, much to their advantage, but to the injury of his health. He saw the importance of the undertaking, persevered through every discouragement to have it accomplished, and by a mighty effort he succeeded[32].

"When I came to this county in 1815 we could only give them preaching on a week day once in two weeks, their faithful friend and ours Mr Wm. McConnell preaching to them on the Sabbath. By considerable extra exertion we gave them Sabbath evenings. The advantage thus afforded was improved and the Society and Congregation were soon considerably increased. The subsequent culture of mission ground in the neighbourhood had a quickening influence and tended still further to advance their interests whilst they continued to increase in life and love.

---

[31] This confirms what Miss McCutcheon says above (page 32) about the difference in social class between the two women.

[32] W J Thompson, in his article in the Irish Christian Advocate of December 1932, recorded that Mr Steele "acted as overseer and labourer at the building of it. He worked with pick and shovel until his hands were blistered, and then worked with gloves on". Mr Steele was stationed in Belfast at the time, so he would have had to ride out to do this work, presumably lodging with one of the congregation.

> "After a few years[33] Mrs Smith had a house built beside the Chapel for a preacher's residence at her own expense. Several of the respectable inhabitants became attached to the congregation and the Society, especially of the "honourable women" who for intelligence, piety and benevolence have been ornaments to their Christian profession.
>
> "Their Sabbath School, Missionary Association and Society Funds are on the increase, while the spiritual and gracious character of the Society, generally speaking, gave satisfactory evidence that "Jesus is the Author and Finisher of their Faith".
>
> "Since the increase referred to at the time of the cholera they have had seasons of sifting and pruning; but they are, thanks be to God, in a healthy and happy state; they are united to each other in affection, and a blessing to their neighbours; they strengthen the hands of their pastors while labouring for their good, and will doubtless be to them "a crown of rejoicing" in the day of Christ."

Kyle tells us that the chapel built in 1813 provided 300 'sittings'. That suggests that the design was state of the art for Methodism at that time. Most chapels in Ireland up till then had no seating. Conference recommended in 1812 that pews should be introduced, because the absence of seating was proving 'a hindrance to respectable families'.

---

[33] Around 1822.

The original trustees, listed in the church's Register of Baptisms and Marriages, are of some interest:

> William McConnell, Grocer, of <Donaghadee>[34]
> Andrew Dalzell, Farmer, of <Donaghadee>
> Thomas Dalzell, Farmer, of Killaghy
> Adam Aldrey, Farmer, of Killaghy[35]
> Adam Averell, Clerk, of <Donaghadee>[36]

---

[34] W J Thompson (*Christian Advocate* 30 Dec 1932) mentions William McConnell along with James Davidson as two of the first Lay Preachers in Donaghadee, and he is also referred to in warm terms by Matthew Lanktree above, and by MacGowan in his *Reminiscences*. Although the Misses Carey and Smith (and other women in that period) are also referred to as having preached they would not have been eligible to be Local Preachers at that date. Conference in Dublin in 1802 resolved:

> "It is the judgment of the Conference, that it is contrary both to Scripture and prudence, that women should either preach or exhort in public, and we direct the superintendents to refuse a society ticket to any woman in the Methodist Connexion who preaches or exhorts in any public congregation, unless she entirely cease from so doing."

The English Conference adopted the same resolution, but by contrast made an exception for women who had 'an extraordinary calling', on condition that they could only preach to their own sex.

[35] Lived near Carrowdore. Reported still alive in 1845.

[36] Rev Adam Averell had been President of the Irish Methodism Conference in 1810. Averell was a deacon in the Church of Ireland ('Clerk in Holy Orders') who resigned his curacy in 1792 and, having independent means, began to engage in a preaching ministry of his own. That same year he attended his first class meeting and seems to have been unofficially associated with Methodism from that time, his name first appearing on the list of stations as a Methodist preacher in 1796. In 1802 he took a lead in the promotion of Sunday Schools, which were then still something of a novelty. He became a leading figure in Conference and was President in 1814. He

BUILDING

>Charles Mayne, Wesleyan Minister[37]
>Thomas W. Doolittle, Wesleyan Minister

A grocer and local preacher, three farmers and three clerics. But it is interesting that the lease was not granted to any of them, but to the patron of the project, Mary Smith. The title page of the copy that survives reads:

>"Dated the 1st day of May 1812
>Daniel Delacherois Esq
>to
>Mrs Mary Smith
>Copy Lease
>of the Wesleyan Chapel, Donaghadee."

The consideration was five shillings and the yearly rent thereafter was to be one shilling. Mary was uniquely well placed to obtain this favourable lease from Daniel Delacherois. The lease states that he granted it to her:

---

ultimately joined the Primitive Wesleyan Methodist Connexion in 1818 of which he was President until his death in 1847.

[37] Rev. Charles Mayne appears in the Rev Hill's memorial as preaching in Donaghadee in 1798 and being instrumental in the conversion of Mary Smith in that year. He was appointed to the Belfast Circuit in 1806, and seems to have been very active, working with Thomas Doolittle, in raising money for new chapels. He opened the Carrickfergus chapel, for example, in November 1812. Doolittle was stationed at Seymour St, Lisburn, in 1811 and 1812, so may have been part of the connection to Mrs Gayer, though Mary Smith would have known her anyway through the family connection in Lisburn.

> "in consideration of the yearly rents, covenants, clauses, conditions and agreements *and also of the esteem and regard which he beareth to his cousin* the said Mary Smith".

The land in question was defined as:

> "all that piece or parcel of ground in the Mound Street ... bounded by tenements in the possession of William Brown and Moses Wright containing in front to said street fifty-nine feet between the said tenements and extending back in the rere 98 feet on Moses Wright's side and 90 feet on Wm Brown's side".

Not only did the main subscriptions to the building of the chapel come from women, but several local women are cited as having been leading spirits in the early years of the church. In addition to Miss Smith and Miss Carey we hear of Mrs Hull, the wife of a retired Major in the British Army, who lived in Rose Bank[38]; Mrs McMinn of the High Street, whose family were to play an important part in the life of the church for several generations[39], Mrs Barnsley and Mrs Marianne Semphill[40].

---

[38] She was the mother of Thomas Hull, see page 59.

[39] The family was to provide a local Magistrate in the next generation. Mrs McMinn lived to 93, almost rivalling Mary Carey's 96 year longevity. Another example of longevity was Mrs McCracken, whose husband hosted the original Methodist class founded by John Hill in Portavo in 1816. MacGowan says that she was "a happy and consistent Christian, who, after the death of her husband, resided with her daughter, Mrs Norwell, in Dongahadee" and died at the age of 92.

BUILDING

Mrs McMinn, like Mary Carey, was one of the very early members of the Society who lived long enough to be captured in a photograph

Mary Smith, 1772-1853

The record states that: "at that time there were few men connected with the society in Donaghadee, and the duty was laid on Mrs Mary Smith to take charge of the chapel funds".[41]

---

[40] Rev R M Morrison, *Christian Advocate* 10 Dec 1902. The names would appear to be taken from the *Reminiscences* published by John MacGowan in 1884. Mrs Semphill could be the widow or daughter in law of the Mr Semphill who, with Marie Angelique Delacherois, founded the Mount Alexander school in Donaghadee in 1771. James Boswell, incidentally, had dinner with both of them in 1769 - another indication of the close involvement of the Establishment in the setting up of the Methodist Church in Donaghadee.

[41] Donaghadee always had a slightly reduced male population, because so many of its men were seafarers; and at that period, in the Napoleonic wars, more men than usual would have been away.

Mary Smith is so important to the founding of the Methodist Church in Donaghadee that it is worth saying a little more about her life and work, which are celebrated by a plaque[42] at the back of the church:

> SACRED
> TO THE MEMORY OF
> MRS. MARY SMITH.
> THIS TABLET IS ERECTED BY A FEW FRIENDS
> WHO CHERISH THE RECOLLECTION OF HER MANY EXCELLENCIES.
> TO HER SELF-DENYING AND GENEROUS EFFORTS
> THE METHODIST CHURCH IS CHIEFLY INDEBTED FOR THIS PLACE OF WORSHIP,
> THE ADJOINING SCHOOL-HOUSE AND PREMISES, AND THE RESIDENCE OF THE MINISTER.
> HER DEEP PIETY, HER CONSISTENT WALK,
> AND HER UNWEARIED BENEVOLENCE TO THE POOR AND AFFLICTED
> DESERVE TO BE HELD IN EVERLASTING REMEMBRANCE.
> SHE FELL ASLEEP IN JESUS ON THE 31ST DECEMBER, 1853,
> AGED 80 YEARS.
> HER SACRED DUST LIES IN THE ADJACENT CEMETERY,
> IN SURE AND CERTAIN HOPE OF A RESURRECTION
> TO ETERNAL LIFE.

Mary was born in Lisburn in 1772 to parents of high social status. She had two younger sisters, Anne and Sarah. Through her mother, Judith, she was connected to the Delacherois family, who were the landowners of Donaghadee. If her mother was actually a Delacherois by birth - as seems likely, because Daniel calls Mary 'cousin' and Judith was a Delacherois family name - then she would have been a considerable heiress

---

[42] The plaque was erected in June, 1888, at the instigation of the Rev Thomas Hull.

and her husband must have been a prominent figure in commerce to have married her.

Mary's family moved from Lisburn to Donaghadee, and stayed there until her father died, after which her mother and sisters returned to Lisburn but she remained in Donaghadee with her brother Michael, who "held important offices, in which he succeeded his father" – probably trading in linen. Her mother and other members of her family joined the Methodist Church in Lisburn about this time (early 1790s), coming under the wing of Mrs Dorothea Johnson, who was to be a lasting influence on Mary too[43].

---

[43] See, for example, Mary Smith's diary, page 96 below. Dorothea Johnson is one of the women celebrated in Crookshank's *Memorable Women of Irish Methodism* (1882). Adam Averell wrote a memoir of her in, which included several of her letters to the Smith sisters in Donaghadee and several poems. This poem 'To Miss S - , L.' appears to have been written to the young Mary Smith when she was still living in Lisburn:

> "Beauteous, lovely, charming maid,
> Soon that lovely form must fade,
> All that beauty die away,
> All lie mouldering in the clay.
> If thou would'st forever bloom,
> Beautiful beyond the tomb,
> Fly the gay unthinking crowd,
> Shun the ways of all the proud.
> Seek in prayer thyself to know,
> Love in wisdom's path to go.
> Let not fashion make thee stray,
> Choose betimes the better way."

As a young woman Mary enjoyed the lively social life of Lisburn and Donaghadee, but she reached a turning point[44] in 1798, when she was 26. Two Ministers, the Rev Samuel Wood and the Rev Charles Mayne, were visiting preachers to Donaghadee

---

Born in 1732, Dorothea's father was a Dutch trader in Dublin who fell into debt and virtually sold her to his creditor, a thoroughly unpleasant man named King. She was unhappily married, apparently with no children, until he died. She then, in 1784, at the age of 52, married the distinguished preacher the Rev John Johnson, who moved to Lisburn and became supernumerary there on grounds of ill-health (he was to die in 1803). John Wesley thought very highly of her. When she was moving from Dublin to Lisburn he wrote, "Tell Sister Gayer, I send her such a sister as she never had before". And in 1785 he wrote that the Lisburn Society, "was the liveliest Society he had seen for many days, owing chiefly to the good providence of God, in bringing Sister Johnson hither". She gathered round her a large number of young women, of whom Mary Smith was one. In 1811, 60 members of the Lisburn Society were under her care. She was apparently a great beauty in her youth, and 'retained the bloom and loveliness of youth' into old age. She died in 1818.

[44] Was she disappointed in love? She was an attractive, intelligent and high spirited young woman with money, and by her own confession a reader of romantic novels, who could not have been short of proposals of marriage. Had she lost a fiancé in the wars? Or, more intriguingly, given the date, was her lover one of the United Irishmen who died that year – possibly even one of those who fell defending Donaghadee Barracks against Crown forces? Perhaps she felt herself to have been spiritually married to him, so that when he was killed she started to call herself 'Mrs', adopted Methodist dress as a proxy for widow's clothes (since it would have been a scandal if she had mourned him openly), and did not put herself up for marriage any more, leaving polite society for the company of the 'poor and despised' Methodists and devoting herself to good works in the spirit of the radicalism he had espoused? The barracks she purchased for a manse in 1836 would have had a special significance for her if his blood had been shed there. But this is all speculation fit for a historical romance, and it has no place in a history. Certainly her memorialist, the Rev Hill, had no inkling of it: but then he did not meet her until 1816, when he was still very young and she was already 44.

from Belfast. The place of worship was the little barn at the rear of Antony Carey's house. She accepted an invitation from Mary Carey (who was her exact contemporary) to attend, and after the service, which moved her greatly, she asked to stay behind and speak to the Rev Mayne. That was the beginning of her association with Methodism.

We have extracts from her diary preserved by Rev John Hill, a selection of which are reproduced at Appendix 1. They show her intense spirituality, which was a driving force of the church for the best part of fifty years. Hill says that the members of the Methodist Society in Donaghadee in this early period were "poor and despised", so joining them must have been at a considerable cost to the young socialite.

> "She ceased to be conformed to the world, and her fashionable apparel was changed for the plain attire by which the Methodists in those days were distinguished."

She reached a particular spiritual crisis in 1809, as recorded in her diary (reproduced at Appendix 1 below), after which she dedicated herself with new vigour to serve Christ. Dorothea Johnson wrote to Mary and her younger sister Anne several times at this critical period in Mary's life. In 1808 she had written to Anne:

> "I am glad you have met with the dear people of God, and found freedom ... Please give my love to your sister (Mary) and tell her her *half religion* will never make her happy. Unless she yields to the strivings of the Holy Spirit and to

the light of her conscience she *must* be miserable: no man can serve two masters."

By then Anne had come to live with her in Donaghadee, and they spent the rest of their lives together, neither of them ever marrying but eventually settling down to live in a house with Mary Carey. We are told that since they were both 'Miss Smith' the elder was distinguished by being called 'Mrs'[45]. They were both extremely pious women, and Hill composed memorials to honour each of them.

In 1811 Dorothea wrote to Mary:

> "I feel it must have been painful to paint so clear a view as you give of your fallen nature, but bad as it is, there is a remedy for all your ills. It was the enemy's grand device, to hinder you from private prayer, by suggesting to you the common temptation, that you had committed the unpardonable sin. He doth not thus attack those he is secure of.
>
> "Never be ashamed of owning Him in his despised people, in this proud world let His word be your constant rule."

---

[45] There is something odd about this. On the continent an unmarried woman starts to be called 'Frau' or 'Madame' when she reaches a certain age, but as devotees of Jane Austen will know, the practice in England at that time was that the eldest daughter was called 'Miss Bennet' and the others were 'Miss Elizabeth', 'Miss Mary' etc. So the natural way to distinguish the two Misses Smith would have been as 'Miss Smith' and 'Miss Anne'. Mary was too young to start being called Mrs Smith on grounds of age, hence the suggestion in the previous footnote.

BUILDING

And a few months later, with admiration:

"What has He wrought in you, your mother and sisters?"

The spiritual reinforcement Mrs Johnson gave to Mary must have been indispensable to her commitment to the Methodist Society, and therefore to her determination six months later to build a Methodist Chapel in Donaghadee.

Mary was all her life thereafter active in good works about the town. She is described as having:

> "...talents of a high order. Her understanding was vigorous, and richly stored with knowledge. In her personal appearance she was prepossessing, and by constitution and habit formed for exertion".

On one of her visits to Lisburn she called, as has been said, on Mrs Gayer at Lambeg, who made the first financial contribution to the project for building the Methodist Chapel in Donaghadee. As a result, says Hill, "after much labour and anxiety, a large and beautiful chapel was opened for the worship of God".

Later on, probably when she was in her fifties, she suffered a serious accident:

> "While on one of her errands of mercy she got a fearful fall through the trap door of an upper room, down into a cellar. Her escape from being killed was a wonderful display of Divine Providence. However, she sustained

injury, by which the sight of one eye was lost and the other much injured."

After that her activities were curtailed and she suffered further illnesses, including minor strokes, but she still "watched over the classes of females with tender care, and when unable to go abroad, they were brought to her house". She devoted all her remaining worldly wealth to the building of the schoolhouse in 1846 and the rebuilding of the church in 1849. She lived to the age of 80 and continued to have a huge influence on the congregation, even when in her later years she had to be carried to her pew for each service.

Relations with the Established Church

We have already noted that several of the original sponsors of the Donaghadee Chapel were Anglicans. This is not as surprising as it might seem. Prior to 1816 all Methodists were also Anglicans. Strictly, the whole population belonged to the Parish, because the Anglican Church was the Established Church of Ireland; but Methodists were Anglicans in the real sense that they were baptised and took Communion in the Parish Church.

Up till 1845 they also married in the Parish Church, but then a law was passed which allowed marriage in a Methodist Chapel as long as the Registrar was present to do the formalities. In 1863 it became possible to register a Methodist Chapel for marriage and the Methodist Minister became, in effect, the Registrar at such ceremonies. Donaghadee actually has records of some marriages dating back to the 1830s, but presumably they were solemnisations of marriages that had been effected elsewhere.

John Wesley always saw Methodism as a part of the Anglican Church, and until his very last years, when he had effectively lost control of the Connexion, he refused to ordain Methodists to administer the Sacraments, making exceptions only for those who were appointed to minister in countries, like Scotland or America, where the Anglican Church was not represented. People like Daniel Delacherois[46] may have seen Methodism as Anglicanism for the lower classes, rather than as a rival denomination.

That did not mean that Church of Ireland clergy, any more than their counterparts in England and Wales, always *liked* Methodists: Methodism drew attention to the shortcomings in the provision the Established Church was offering to the working class, and very often the enthusiasm of its followers was an embarrassment to them and hard to contain. Lanktree tells how he often had difficult relations with Anglican clergy: he

---

[46] Daniel may also have been sympathetic to Methodism because of his Huguenot roots. His family had been French Protestants who had to flee France after the revocation of the Edict of Nantes in 1685. His grandfather Daniel, with two brothers and two sisters, fled to Holland, where the brothers joined up in the armed forces of William, Prince of Orange, and then came to Ireland to fight with him. Marie Angelique, daughter of the first Daniel's brother Nicholas, became Lady Mount Alexander and inherited the whole of the former Montgomery estates in County Down, which she divided on her death, leaving Donaghadee to Samuel Delacherois, Daniel Jr's father. A Mrs Delacherois was to die a Methodist in Lisburn in 1828.

wanted to be their friend, but was frustrated that they often preached against Methodism.

However, that was all about to change. Already in 1795 the English Conference had adopted a *Plan of Pacification,* under which Methodist preachers were authorised to administer the sacraments. The Irish Conference had resisted that pressure. On three separate occasions, in 1792, 1795 and 1798 it rejected petitions from Lisburn (then the largest Irish Circuit) and elsewhere to allow the administration of the sacraments. The pressure came mainly from the North of Ireland, where members looked to the example of the Presbyterian Church, and many of those who had come in to the Methodist Church had no previous connection with the Church of Ireland. Conference reacted sharply, disciplining Lisburn and expelling 32 of its leaders.

But the issue would not go away. It came up again at the Conference of 1811, and by 1814 it was clear that something would need to be done. The Conference of that year initially voted by a slim majority to allow the administration of the sacraments in carefully circumscribed conditions, but was then persuaded by opponents to put the plan on hold.

It was not until 1816 that an Irish equivalent of the *Plan of Pacification* was adopted. So far from being a pacificatory measure it led to rancorous division and the formation, by 1818, of the schismatic Primitive Wesleyan Methodist Society, which contined to affirm its loyalty to the Established Church. The Primitives were strongest in the West – Tyrone, Cavan and

BUILDING

Monagahan – and less strong in the more Presbyterian-influenced North East of Ireland, but we read that Matthew Lanktree himself, who, as Chairman of the Belfast District in 1815, was one of the early sacrament-givers, agonised and "prayed fervently" before agreeing to a request from one of his congregations to administer the Lord's Supper to them for the first time.[47]

Anglicans may have regarded Methodists more or less kindly before the split, but as it became clear that the Methodists were moving away from them they reacted sharply. In 1815 the Hon and Rev Charles Knox[48] gave a sermon in Armagh Cathedral, later repeated at Auchnacloy, in which he attacked Methodism. He said that:

> "their meetings for Christian experience[49] were equivalent to Popish confession and tended to mental pollution, their

---

[47] The Primitive Methodists at one time had almost a third of the total membership of Irish Methodism. But it was primarily a lay movement, and the majority of the clergy stayed in the original Connexion. For sixty years two separate annual Methodist Conferences were held in Ireland, a Wesleyan Conference and a Primitive Wesleyan Conference. In 1878 the two Connexions were united and, the Wesleyans adopted the principle of lay representation at Conference for the first time, which had been accepted by the Primitive Wesleyans from their inception. All preachers from both Connexions were recognised as being in full connexion with the united Conference.

[48] 'Honorable' because he was the son of a Viscount.

[49] Methodism started in the Holy Club, which Wesley led when he was a student at Oxford. There was a strong emphasis there on the imortance of confessing one's sins to each other, and this carried forward in due course into Wesley's organisation

extemporaneous prayers were expressions of vanity, their preachers proud and ambitious men artfully labouring to perpetuate their system at the expense of genuine Christianity."

The Rev Samuel Steele, who had built Donaghadee's first chapel, rebutted these allegations in what Crookshank describes as "a very able pamphlet"[50]. Knox was obviously using intemperate language, but what he says is interesting as a view of how Methodism was regarded by Anglicans at that time. Anglicans believed in keeping the Commandments and attending Services regularly, but they did not like the 'enthusiasm' of the Methodists or their introspective probing of one another's sins and agonising about whether they were really saved. To the Anglican mind there was something unhealthy and undignified about such preoccupations, and the upper classes did not like being told that they had a heart as sinful as any common person[51].

---

of 'classes' and still more intimate 'bands' of leaders within Methodism. Anyone who aspired to a leadership position had to commit to regularly confessing their sins and accepting reproof from their fellows. Bands disappeared from Methodism around the end of the C 18th.

[50] Crookshank, Vol 2, p.398 ff.

[51] "These doctrines", the Duchess of Buckingham wrote to a friend, "are most repulsive and strongly tinctured with impertinence and disrespect towards their superiors" – something of which the Established Church could not be accused.

As Methodism in Ireland separated from Anglicanism it tended to assimilate more to the Calvinism of the Presbyterian Church here, emphasising its distinction from Anglicanism and giving it a different character from Methodism in England. From being at war with their Presbyterian neighbours in 1798, the local Methodists settled into comfortable proximity as fellow Ulster Protestants.

Methodists and Presbyterians

Doctrinally there is no material difference between the Anglican and Methodist Churches, the main points at issue being the difficulty the Anglicans have in recognising the validity of Methodist ordination (even that has now effectively been surmounted as a result of the recent Covenant) and the difficulty many Methodist clergy would have in taking on the full package of Articles to which a clergyman in the Church of Ireland has to subscribe.

But there is a major doctrinal difference between Anglicans and Methodists on the one side and Presbyterians on the other. Wesley contended all his life against the Calvinist doctrines of preordination and irresistible grace. In 1739 he wrote:

> "There is blasphemy clearly contained in the horrible decree of preordination. And here I fix my foot. And on this I take issue with every assertion to it. You represent God as worse than the Devil. But you say that you will prove by scripture. Hold! It cannot do."

His brother Charles backed him up with these verses:

> "And shall I, Lord, confine they love,
> as not to others free?
> And may not every sinner prove,
> the grace that found out me?
>
> Doom them an endless death to die,
> from which they could not flee?
> O Lord, thine inmost bowels cry,
> against this dire decree."

Anglicans and Methodists, who are known for this purpose as 'Arminians', believe that Jesus died for all sinners, so all can be saved; whereas Calvinists believe that only those pre-selected by God are to be saved. Calvinists defend the complete sovereignty of God, and therefore argue that a person's salvation must depend on God's election alone. So it was not surprising that there was antagonism when Methodism appeared in the predominantly Presbyterian areas of Ireland. However, Methodism had started as an association of independent revivalist societies many of which were Calvinist, and if Wesley personally had not been so determined to stay within the Anglican Church Methodism could easily have become a Calvinist sect.

Indeed, some branches of Methodism actually became Calvinist. The Countess of Huntingdon was much taken with John Wesley's one-time friend and collaborator, George Whitefield, who was a Calvinist, and when Wesley rejected Calvinism at the 1770 Conference she formed her own Connexion. It included the Welsh Calvinistic Methodist Church, which eventually became the Presbyterian Church in Wales. The Countess sent preachers to Ireland, but they did not establish a lasting presence except for the Welsh Chapels in Dublin and Dun Laoghaire, which survived till the outbreak of the Second World War.

As Methodism established itself in Ireland the latent inclination to Calvinism among many of its adherents was reinforced by the influence of the local Presbyterians, from whose numbers some of its new members were drawn and with whose families they frequently intermarried. So in 1814 we already find a leading Methodist commentator (who remained anonymous) suggesting that maybe a moderate admixture of Calvinism in Methodism would be no bad thing. This rapid assimilation made it easier for Northern Methodists to make common cause with Presbyterians politically when it became expedient to do so[52].

---

[52] Rev Matthew Lanktree, who was then engaged in the Down Mission, based in Comber, wrote in 1821 that "the majority of the people [in that area] were Presbyterians, many of them, as well as their Ministers, Arians. Their prejudices against Methodism are greatly diminished". In the early days Methodists often characterised Presbyterians as 'Arians' (i.e. adherents to the Arian heresy that Jesus is similar to, rather than 'of one being with', God the Father) because of their Old Testament emphasis on God the Father, which Methodists felt led them to downplay the importance of the Second Person of the Trinity.

Chapter 4
Rebuilding

The progress of Methodism

Crookshank tells us that, despite the schism, the period around 1816 was an encouraging one for Methodism, whose influence was evidenced by "drunkenness, Sabbath-breaking and profane swearing being everywhere given up". He notes that in the district between Donaghadee and Portaferry there was, in particular, "an extraordinary awakening". In 1820 he records that "Lanktree and Wilson had a good and happy year on the Ards Mission", but that

> "Grey Abbey was a very wicked place and many of the inhabitants were infidels. Mr Lanktree resolved to preach there, though it be at risk to his life".

In the event there seems to have been no trouble[53].

It was also an active time for the proselytising of Catholics. Wesley himself had often addressed gatherings where the majority of those present were Catholics and Irish speakers. He had a famous ability to be 'all things to all men', and is said to have left some of his Catholic audiences wondering whether

---

[53] Lanktree himself has some interesting comments on other places in the area. He speaks of Killaghy (Killaughey) as "long famed for licentiousness", and Ardmillan as "otherwise called 'Little Sodom'".

perhaps he was some sort of Jesuit. His approach was certainly ecumenical.

There was now a distinct mission to convert Catholics led by Ouseley, Noble and others, who preached in Irish. Gideon Ouseley visited Donaghadee in 1816 and preached to large crowds in the open air. The church's Baptismal Roll suggests that Donaghadee Methodist Church benefited from the conversion of Catholics: there are a number of authentic Irish names that appear in the early years among the predominantly Scottish and English names, though one cannot be sure how recently any of those families was Catholic. This proselytisation was to continue for thirty or forty years, and eventually provoked a strong reaction on the part of the Catholic Church, including the burning of the Bibles and tracts that the Methodists handed out.

The first and second manses

In 1821 the 15 year old Thomas Hull (son of Major and Mrs Hull, whom we met above[54]), who was five years later to be accepted as a Methodist Minister[55], first accompanied his mother to services in the Donaghadee chapel. She had been

---

[54] Page 42.

[55] John MacGowan wrote in his *Reminiscences* (1884): "The Rev T.T.N. Hull we would gladly claim as our own; as he was brought up among us, and in early youth began to exercise among us those sanctified talents, and evince that zeal for the extension of Christ's kingdom, which have for so lengthened a period caused him to be a living power for good in the Church and in the world".

converted while in the Isle of Man, and on her return joined the Donaghadee Society, perhaps around the time the chapel was built. We are told that in 1821 there was still no Sunday morning service[56], but only services in the evenings, alternating between preachers from Newtownards and a Local Preacher from Bangor, a Sergeant, who used to preach in full regimental dress[57].

The Rev T T N Hull, about 1860

---

[56] This is surprising if true, because the Minutes of Conference show the Rev David Waugh appointed to Donaghadee in 1820. It may be that Crookshank is in error here, and the whole story is to be dated earlier.

[57] Crookshank Vol 3, p.236

REBUILDING

It was in 1821 that Donaghadee and Newtownards, according to Lanktree, "were formed into a *regular* Circuit for two preachers", and Donaghadee makes its first appearance in the Minutes of Conference in that year, showing a membership of 332 for the Circuit as a whole.

The Rev John Hill writes that:

> "A good chapel having been provided, made the want of a sufficient supply of ministerial aid to be the more felt by the people. The circumstances of the ministers prevented them from meeting the needs of the Donaghadee Society, it being an outpost of the Belfast circuit, on which were stationed only two ministers, and they had to visit seven towns, besides country places.....
>
> "The revival of the good work made it needful to form a new circuit, of which Donaghadee was the principal place[58]. This made it necessary to provide a house in which the minister should dwell; and to secure the residence, and a full supply of labour, [Mrs Smith] had a house erected on the chapel premises at her own cost."

---

[58] That happened in 1820. If there was no manse and no Minister in residence in 1821, as Crookshank suggests (above), then the first manse must have been built very soon after, say in 1822.

The first Minister of the new Circuit was the Rev Alexander Sturgeon, of whom and his successors John MacGowan writes[59]:

> "The Rev Alexander Sturgeon came to Donaghadee in 1821, and remined three years. He was one of the most gentle of men – a gentleman in every sense – and his family were most amiable. After him came the Rev William Keys, and after him the Rev Michael Burrows, both excellent men. In 1828 the Rev Thomas Ballard came to this Circuit. He was a man of ability and zeal, and a fearless champion for the truths of the Gospel. Mrs Ballard was one of the best and wisest women I have known.
>
> "After Mr Ballard we had the Rev Samuel Harpur, a most gentle and amiable man. It was in the year 1832 that Donaghadee was favoured with a visit from the celebrated Dr Adam Clarke[60]. He had come to spend a few days with Mr Harpur, for whom he had a sincere affection. During Dr Clarke's short stay he preached two or three times in our chapel".

Dr Clarke was to die two months later, and Samuel Harpur also fell ill.

---

[59] *Reminiscences,* p.15

[60] Dr Clarke enjoyed celebrity status in Methodism at that time. We are told that women would treasure locks of his silver hair which he would cut off for them.

REBUILDING

In 1832 Donaghadee was struck by an outbreak of cholera, which is vividly described by Matthew Lanktree (see Appendix 2). Lanktree had returned to Donaghadee hoping to enjoy a quiet time (because he was beginning to feel his age) in the agreeable company of his friend, the Rev Samuel Harpur. But Harpur became ill soon after he arrived, and he was left to cope with the cholera epidemic on his own. Scores of people died, but the effect on the church was positive. The imminent threat of death concentrated people's minds, and church attendance increased so much that two new galleries had to be built to accommodate the extra numbers.

The second manse was built in 1836, and was called 'Wesley Lodge'. Mary Smith purchased the old military barracks on the Millisle Road, on the site of the present 7 Millisle Road, for £71, with the intention that they would provide a more spacious manse. When they did not prove suitable, she had them demolished and built a new manse at her own expense, which served until 1893, when a third manse, called 'Epworth', was built on the same site[61]. Wesley Lodge was large enough to include a room for a visiting or junior preacher and a room for the (by now elderly) Mary Carey, who had been forced out of her father's house following his death. Miss McCutcheon, in the letter quoted above[62], says that Miss Carey had two self-

---

[61] That 1893 building is still there at 7 Millisle Road, though it ceased to be the manse in 1969, when the name of 'Epworth' was transferred to 64 Millisle Road. The manse moved to Breckenridge in 2009.

[62] Page 32.

contained rooms in the manse, one of which was let to the junior Minister, whom she looked after.

The Great Famine

The Great Famine of 1845 to 1851 is the defining event in the history of Ireland in the 19th Century[63]. More than a million people starved to death and more than a million emigrated in just five years. But it was only the sharpest manifestation of the distress of Ireland throughout the century, in the course of which Ireland's population fell from over eight million to four and a half million. It is impossible to exaggerate the poverty and the wretched condition of most of the population of Ireland at that time. Even before the famine there had been countless Royal Commissions set up by the British Government to investigate the problem. But though the Penal Laws had been repealed in 1793 and there was Catholic emancipation in 1829

---

[63] Although Crookshank goes on to note with approval the measures Methodists took to assist with relief work, he cannot be forgiven for the way in which he regarded the famine as, in a sense, providential:

> "In the heart of the nation [in 1847] the spirit of disloyalty smouldered, like a pent-up fire, only waiting to burst forth in the lurid flames of rebellion and murder. ... Popery had laid her plans and was watching the opportunity to deluge the country with blood. Her fell spirit was burning in the hearts and frowning in the countenances of millions of her deluded votaries, when God Himself interposed a judgement. This Divine visitation was, no doubt, the means of saving the country from the curse of a most fatal civil war."

He was presumably not alone in regarding the death of a million of his countrymen as possibly no bad thing. In tenuous mitigation, Crookshank was writing in the 1880s, at a time of heightened anti-Catholic feeling (see page 79 below).

the condition of the peasantry continued to be appalling. The root of the problem was the system of land tenure, in which most land was owned by absentee landlords in England, who visited their properties rarely (not surprisingly, since they took their lives in their hands when they did so) and left the management of them to 'middlemen', who exploited the tenant farmers ruthlessly[64].

However, this distress in most of Ireland affected Donaghadee comparatively little. Tenant farmers in Ulster fared better than their counterparts in Leinster, Munster and Connaught because they benefitted from tenants' rights, whereas farmers elsewhere were 'tenants at will' and could be evicted at any time. Moreover Belfast and Bangor were industrialising and growing at a time when the rest of Ireland was shrinking. Donaghadee and the Ards were still very poor by our standards, and as Harry Allen says, the women folk had to help make ends meet by a cottage industry of embroidery or 'flowering', but they were not starving like the rest of Ireland. When there was a resumption of militancy in 1849 with the rebellion of the Young Irishmen it barely touched this part of Ulster.

In 1849 the Donaghadee to Portpatrick steam packet service ceased, which was a grave blow to the town. The building of the

---

[64] The problem of absentee landlords and rural impoverishment was not confined to Ireland. Ever since the Industrial Revolution in the 18th century people had been literally starving to death in the English countryside, and even more so in Scotland. But the problem was more acute in Ireland and went unnoticed for longer, because there were fewer industrial centres into which the unemployed could migrate.

railway from Belfast in 1861 was, in part, an attempt to get it reinstated, but that was not to happen. Donaghadee therefore ceased to be a passenger port, and the hotels along the front turned to the holiday trade brought by the railway as the mainstay of their business. The harbour was still busy with fishing boats and ships bringing coal, which was unloaded on to railway wagons on the pier, but the character of the town had changed from commercial to residential and recreational.

Donaghadee had to compete with Bangor, too, which overtook it in size at this time. Bangor did not get its railway until 1865, but when it did it was able to offer a quicker connection to Belfast – 12 miles on the railway, as against 22 miles to Donaghadee – and it leapt ahead as a destination for day trippers and for commuters. Donaghadee became a bit of a backwater, though the hotels survived well in to the next century and desirable residential property began to spread along the Warren Road and the Millisle Road within walking distance of the railway station. So what was the Church doing in this period?

The new school (1846) and the rebuilding of the church (1849)

One of the measures the Government took to improve the condition of the poor was the institution of National Schools, starting in 1831. Donaghadee's first National School was founded in 1839 on Schoolhouse Brae. It was followed by Bow Lane National School in 1840, the ruins of which are still standing behind the Market House on New Street. But then the

REBUILDING

various churches decided that they too wanted a role in education. First Presbyterian opened a school in what is now the Curragh Room, and then the Methodists built their School House in 1846, together with a house for the schoolteacher next to the church. Hill writes:

> "A school was considered to be much wanted, where the children of our people could obtain a suitable education. For this purpose ground was taken adjoining the chapel, and by the careful attention of the Rev William Cather, a good house was erected, containing large school-rooms, and accommodation for the teacher. Mrs Barnsley and Miss Smith[65] generally lent their aid to [Mary Smith] in the accomplishment of these important undertakings. Other kind friends also helped, and they had the pleasure of seeing a good school in operation..."

William Cather was the Minister at Donaghadee 1845 – 1847. He seems to have been made trustee of a fund of £150, invested in Belfast Harbour Board stock, the interest on which – about £6 a year - paid the ground rent for the school. In 1877 the Quarterly Board resolved that:

> "the Revd Oliver McCutcheon [Minister at the time] write to the Revd William Cather for information relative to the sum of £150 now in the hands of the Belfast Harbour Board, the interest on which is payable

---

[65] The younger sister, Anne.

> to the teacher of the National School ... to meet the annual rent of school premises."

The church was itself completely rebuilt in 1849, and it is the 1849 structure that is the basic shell of the present church building, though it was added to and substantially re-modelled in 1909. The church was not merely growing in numbers, but was also advancing in terms of the social composition of its members, as can be seen from the Baptismal Roll discussed in Appendix 2. By the middle of the century Methodism had become middle class as well as working class, but with a continuing strong commitment to the less advantaged in society.

The Donaghadee Chapel, the Old Manse[66] and the Schoolhouse all appear in a Deed of Trust dated 7 May 1850, the names on which were:

for the Chapel:	Mary Smith;
for the Old Manse:	Mary Smith and others, and
for the Schoolhouse:	Rev John Hill and others.

Mary Smith was by then 77 years old, practically blind, disabled and an invalid, yet it was still her name on the papers. She had completed her service to the Church, and was to die three years later. In 40 years she had built two chapels, two manses and a schoolhouse, of which the second chapel (1849) and the schoolhouse (1846) form the main church buildings to this day.

---

[66] i.e. the 1822 manse, which served a variety of purposes until it was demolished to make room for the 1909 church redevelopment.

Chapter 5
The spirit of the age

The revival of 1859

In 1859 there was a Methodist revival which affected Donaghadee and the Ards. Crookshank writes[67]:

> "At Donaghadee the first token of the coming shower was in the Wesleyan Sunday School, where there was a blessed manifestation of the presence and power of the Holy Spirit. A young woman was affected to bodily weakness (i.e. fainted), and the work thus begun soon spread until the town was in a blaze.
>
> "On Sunday in Newtownards while the Rev Wm Brown was preaching a woman started to her feet and shouted, "Jesus is here, Jesus is here". She was removed by the leaders to the school room, but soon another and another had to be taken away, until preaching had to give way to prayer and praise."

Though commentators tend to focus on the more sensational incidents like these, there is evidence that there was a substantial and lasting effect of the revival. The Methodist Church and the Presbyterian Church too grew by several thousand members

---

[67] Crookshank Vol 3, p.516

over the next few years. The Rev. Kyle's history reflects this in Donaghadee:

> "As an illustration of the work in Donaghadee, in the year 1857 there were 93 members[68]; in 1860 131 members and in 1861 153 members. In 1863 there were 93 scholars in Sunday School, also 14 scholars in Sunday School on Copeland Island".

There were also, in 1864, 83 scholars in the Day School and another 12 on Copeland Island.

The start of the modern era: the 1860s and 1870s

The 1860s were a period of rising prosperity in Northern Ireland. Agriculture and industry both prospered. The interruption of cotton supplies due to the American Civil War gave a boost to the local linen industry. Belfast was booming and throwing up splendid commercial and civic buildings of which, sadly, only a few have survived. At the same time there was great poverty in the city, and the City Mission was running shelters for the homeless and so-called 'Arab schools' for the destitute children known as 'street Arabs'. It was able to do that, greatly to its credit, because the middle class, which by now constituted the backbone of Methodism, was doing rather well.

---

[68] The congregation would have been considerably larger. The original chapel had seating for 300, and had been expanded by the addition of galleries in 1832. The 1849 chapel may have had room for as many as 500.

Methodists were becoming better educated, and were beginning to grapple with the issues being thrown up by thinkers in Britain and on the Continent, such as the implications of the fossil record for the literal truth of the Creation story, and the development of Biblical text criticism. The newspaper the *Christian Evangelist* first appeared in 1859, and by 1869 for the first time examinations, oral and written, were required for candidates for the Ministry. The Methodist College in Belfast was founded in 1868 to ensure that young Methodists kept up with the best of their peers intellectually.

As we have seen (page 50), from 1863 Methodist Ministers were allowed to conduct marriages in their chapels without a Registrar needing to be there to validate the proceedings. It is an important token of the extent to which Methodism had by then come of age and become an official church.

The Rev John Greer, Minister in 1869-70, was a noted orator[69]

---

[69] He died suddenly, we are told, before he was able to write up the Register of Baptisms and Marriages.

Funerals were an issue up to this time, because the Parish graveyard had an effective monopoly for burials: there were as yet no cremations or municipal cemeteries. But that was soon to change.

By 1870 the town of Newtownards had outstripped Donaghadee in size, and its Methodist societies outnumbered Donaghadee's by two to one. Newtownards felt that it should become the head of the Circuit, but there was a reluctance to demote Donaghadee, so the solution was to make Donaghadee a separate, one-church Circuit. In the process it became weaker both financially and in terms of Ministerial resources, and its unusual status as a one-church Circuit was often to have an influence thereafter on the selection of Ministers for the station.

Temperance

John Wesley was not a total abstainer. He drank beer regularly (he preferred it sweet rather than made bitter with hops) and he liked a glass of wine, though there were times in his life when he abstained from it. His opposition was to spirits – 'the dram' – which, like many other observers in his day, he saw as a cause of ill-health and misery among the poor.

From about 1830 there was a movement for Temperance, i.e. moderation in the consumption of alcohol, which soon turned into a movement for total abstention.

The first Bands of Hope were set up in the 1850s, and Temperance was a repeated theme in the proceedings of Conference in that decade, so it is likely that Donaghadee first had a Band of Hope around that time. Up till 1878 the Methodist Church followed the Anglican practice of using port wine for Communion, but with the growing emphasis on total abstinence there was a move to have it substituted with unfermented grape juice. In 1875 Conference refused "to condemn that which God has not condemned", but three years later it gave in to the pressure from the Temperance movement and agreed that grape juice could be allowed to be served alongside wine.

Temperance continued to be a major theme up till the Great War[70]. In 1896 there were 333 on the roll of the local Temperance Association. They held services on Sunday afternoons and once a week on a weekday evening in a new hall built at the expense of Mr John Ferguson of Moor Farm, one of the Methodist Church Trustees. In 1903 a hall or preaching room was lent to them in Ballygrainey for occasional services. In 1907 they noted sternly that:

> "There is efficient Temperance Teaching on scientific lines in the Day School more rational and to the point than the ordinary programmes of the Variety Entertainment commonly called a Band of Hope meeting".

---

[70] It received fresh impetus in 1909, when the 'Catch my Pal' movement was started in Belfast.

Music

It is likely that Donaghadee would have gained its first harmonium to accompany worship around the 1860s. Before then, there was no use of pianos or other keyboards in Methodist chapels. Most singing was led by a precentor, with occasional use of a fiddle or cornet to strike up the tune. Methodism in Ireland got its first organ in Centenary Church, Dublin, in 1869, followed by Carlisle Memorial Church in Belfast, built in 1876, but it was not until 1923 that Donaghadee Methodist acquired an organ.

In the first half of the century Methodist hymn books existed but there were no hymn books in general use. In Donaghadee they first came in in the late 1870s, or more likely the 1880s. It was not until around 1870 that there was wide enough literacy to make the use of hymn books possible in most Methodist churches in Ireland[71]. The practice everywhere up to then was 'lining', in which the leader would give the congregation two lines at a time, which they would then sing.

In 1875 Ira Sankey and Dwight Moody made their first visit to Belfast, and a meeting in Botanic Gardens attracted over 50,000 people. Sankey's *Songs and Solos,* designed to accompany the evangelistic missions of Dwight Moody, were a major influence on Methodism in this period. Sankey's book never replaced the Methodist Hymn Book in services, but it was used in smaller

---

[71] The 1861 census showed that only 45 per cent of Irish Methodists could read and write (but that was the highest proportion of any denomination).

THE SPIRIT OF THE AGE

meetings and particularly in the homes of Methodist people. D L Cooney notes that Moody was "weak on theology and strong on sentiment", and that the use of Sankey's book brought about a subtle change in Methodist piety. Methodists, he says,

> "had learned their theology by singing the hymns of Charles Wesley; but now theology began to give way to sentiment".[72]

Church life in the 1870s and 1880s

In 1874 the pattern of weekly church activities was as follows:

> Sabbath Morning Class in the Old Manse at 10am.
> Morning Service at 11am.
> Mid-day class in Schoolroom at 12.30pm.
> Afternoon class in back Schoolroom at 3.45pm.
> Monday evening class after prayer meeting.
> Tuesday evening class in Church at 7pm.

A couple of resolutions of the Leaders' Meeting in 1875 are worth recording:

> "Resolved, that in future the collection for the Poor be taken up after Morning Service on Love Feast days[73], so

---

[72] The Billy Graham campaigns in England in the 1960s likewise produced a hymn book, *Mission Praise,* which has come into regular use alongside *Hymns and Psalms* and is now threatening to displace the official Methodist hymnbook.

[73] This proved successful, and contributions to the poor increased to £1.63 on the next Love Feast day. The Poor Fund regularly supported about eight to ten people

> those of the Congregation who do not wait for the Love Feast may have an opportunity of contributing."

> "Resolved, that the Home Mission Fund Committee be asked to grant an additional ten pounds to the Donaghadee Circuit upon the condition that the Circuit make up another ten pounds so that the Minister's salary may be £120."

There is also a note in the records for 1877 that:

> "There is an orphan maintained at the expense of the Orphan Society, his name is John Gillespie, he lives with his aunt, Elizabeth Hudson, in the Back Street (i.e. Manor Street). The sum of 30/- is allowed per quarter, of which 27/6 is given to his aunt and 2/6 to Mr Morrison for his schooling".

In the same year the church said farewell to the Rev Robert Jamison:

> "We the Leaders and Stewarts[74] of the Donaghadee Circuit have great pleasure in testifying to the kindness of our pastor the Revd Robert Jamison and to his diligence and faithfulness in the discharge of his

---

at that time, who would typically get 2/6d each. One Love Feast and one Sacrament of Holy Communion was held each quarter. Love Feasts were characterised by the giving of personal testimony (see footnote 20 on page 29).

[74] That was the usual spelling at that period.

pastoral duties. He leaves the Circuit with the sincere esteem and love of the Society".

A note in the Circuit Schedules for 1880 describes the pattern of work at the time:

> "The Class is met in the school room after Sermon on Sunday by the Minister; and their Class is met in the Church by Thomas Mork; and another in School Room by Mrs Robertson. The Sunday School is held at half past two o'clock. There is a Teacher's preparation class in the Superintendent's house (Mr Morrison) every Monday evening at 8 o'clock. John Gordon conducts his Class every Tuesday evening after the Sermon. Several cottage services are held by the Leaders through the town on Sunday evenings at 5 o'clock, and on other week evenings at half past 7. Mr McGowan got leave at last Leaders' Meeting to change his Class and prayer meeting from Friday to Monday evening".

The Minister usually preached four or five sermons a week, three in Donaghadee and one or two elsewhere such as Carrowdore, Ballymaconnell, Ballyblack or Gransha.

In 1882 the Leaders resolved:

> "that a new roof is required for the Chapel, the present roof being in a dilapidated state, and that an effort be made to put a new roof on the chapel and some other improvements made which are not yet decided upon."

The 'other improvements' were agreed at the next meeting "that it be newly cleaned and painted, and a lamp placed in front of it". The chapel was re-roofed and throughly renovated at a cost of £125.

In 1888 the memorial tablet to Mrs Mary Smith was erected in the church. The inscription was written by the Rev T T N Hull, who contributed a third of the total cost of £18.

This photograph is of uncertain date, perhaps around 1880. It shows the church and the school under a single roof. The church is recognisable by its three windows with two doors under the windows at each side. The road is not yet surfaced, and there is no pavement in front of the church.

Chapter 6
The end of the era

Home Rule

It was in the 1870's that the agitation for Home Rule[75] began. Agriculture went through a bad period in the late 70s and early 80s: there was a famine in 1879, and around 10,000 evictions between 1874 and 1887, leading to a great deal of violence on the land, with reprisals led by 'Captain Moonlight', as the bands of marauders were known.

Gladstone's response to this was, first, to legislate for fair rents and fixity of tenure in 1881; and then, in 1885, he declared in favour of Home Rule and introduced his first Home Rule Bill.

Thereupon sectarian rioting erupted in Belfast, especially on the Falls and the Shankill, and Protestants rallied, adopting the slogans "Home Rule will be Rome Rule" and (first used by Lord Randolph Churchill) "Ulster will fight, and Ulster will be right". Protestant fears were not entirely unfounded. In this period, and right up to the Great War, the Catholic Church strongly asserted its claim to Ireland as a Catholic country[76], and there

---

[75] That is, for devolved government for the whole of Ireland within the United Kingdom, on the lines of the arrangements eventually agreed for the Stormont Parliament and the current Legislative Assembly.

[76] Catholic assertiveness culminated in the application to Ireland of the *Ne temere* decree in 1908, under which mixed marriages were to be given very shabby

was at that time no framework of institutions, such as exists today, to ensure that one community could not make it a cold house for the other.

Rev R M Morrison was Minister at Donaghadee 1884-86

Anti-Catholic feeling was running high in Methodism at this time. Nevertheless some Methodists, even in the midst of sectarian rioting, tried to hold to the Wesleyan principle of being 'friends of all and enemies of none', and the Wesleyan Chapel on the Falls Road survived remarkably untouched.

---

treatment: a clear indication that the country as a whole was expected to be Catholic.

THE END OF THE ERA

The third manse and the reshaping of the church

In 1893 a new manse called 'Epworth'[77] was built on the site of the old manse, Wesley Lodge, at a cost of £713 6s 0d.

The decision to build a new manse was taken in 1891, Wesley Lodge being by then in a very poor state of repair. Rev Kyle says:

> "It was... resolved that the action of the Rev Mr Johnston in enlisting the services of ladies from Belfast and elsewhere, and their promise to give their best efforts for the raising of funds to build a new manse in Donaghadee, has the hearty approval of this meeting."

The ladies did not let them down. A New Manse Bazaar was held in St George's Hall in Belfast the following year, with a wide variety of stalls, which raised £550 on the day and £600 by the time all the donations had come in[78]. Below is a picture of 'Epworth' when it was newly built.

The original Old Manse (adjacent to the church and dating from about 1822) was then rented to Mr William Morrison, Senior

---

[77] John Wesley was born in the Rectory at Epworth in Lincolnshire. His father, the Rev Samuel Wesley, founded the Epworth Society, the rules of which were in some ways a forerunner of Methodism.

[78] *Christian Advocate*, 2 Dec 1892, p.603. The sum would equate to more than £60,000 in today's money. Nevertheless there was in addition a Glebe Loan on the manse, which was not paid off until 1930.

Circuit Steward, who had just retired from teaching after an active service of about 45 years, at a rent of £8 a year, and the Teacher's Residence was handed over to Mr Mayes. Alexander Mayes was School Superintendent from 1893 to 1895, followed by Robert Hull (1896-1897), Charles H Johnston (1898-1901) and Arthur McMillan (1901-1916).

NEW METHODIST MANSE, DONAGHADEE.

The manse of 1893

In 1897 the Day School had a roll of 83, with average attendance of 58; while the Sunday School had a roll of 134, with attendance of 86. That year the church spent £3.40 on books for the Sunday School and £2.43 for the children's Tea Meeting. The church paid for one orphan, Alice Davis, to attend both schools.

THE END OF THE ERA

Soon after the manse was completed, the Church Leaders turned their minds to rebuilding the church and school. In 1898 Conference voted to raise a 'Twentieth Century Fund' of £50,000 "for aggressive work at the start of the new century", and in 1899 no less than £52,630 was in fact raised, with the intention that it should go into new buildings[79], schools and missions. That spirit, and the knowledge that there were funds available, inspired Donaghadee to make its plans. An article in the *Christian Advocate* in December 1902 said:

> "The fact that this chapel has stood for so long, and even now shows scarcely any signs of decay, proves [that it was well built and well cared for[80].] Nevertheless... the time sems to have come for it to give place to another building, better adapted to present needs and more in accordance with the increasing importance of Donaghadee as a health resort and watering place. The project for a new church has been much discussed and a plan for the building was even selected a short time ago, but the scheme fell through. We trust, however, ... that the many who take an interest in the Methodists of Donaghadee will rally round the cause ... so that in future years the families of our people who may visit Donaghadee ... will find sufficient room and not be under any necessity of worshipping elsewhere."

---

[79] No less than 14 chapels were built or rebuilt in the following ten years.

[80] The writer seems to have thought it was the original 1813 chapel, unaware that it had been rebuilt in 1849.

MÉTHODIST CHAPEL AND SCHOOLROOM, DONAGHADEE.

The church in 1902, with its twin doors opening straight on to the street. The entrance to the Old Manse is on the left, and the schoolhouse on the right

It is clear that the church was doing well and needed extra accommodation for worshippers visiting from Belfast; clear, also, that the church was counting on financial support from Belfast as well as from central Methodism.

As soon as the decision to proceed was taken a general appeal was put out for help both from the Connexion and from Belfast Methodists for a new church "in a watering place so largely frequented by them every season".

The Rev George Wedgewood, Chairman of the Property Board, recommended that a new site should be obtained, but the local church leaders thought otherwise and their view prevailed.

DONAGHADEE NEW CHURCH AND SCHOOLS.

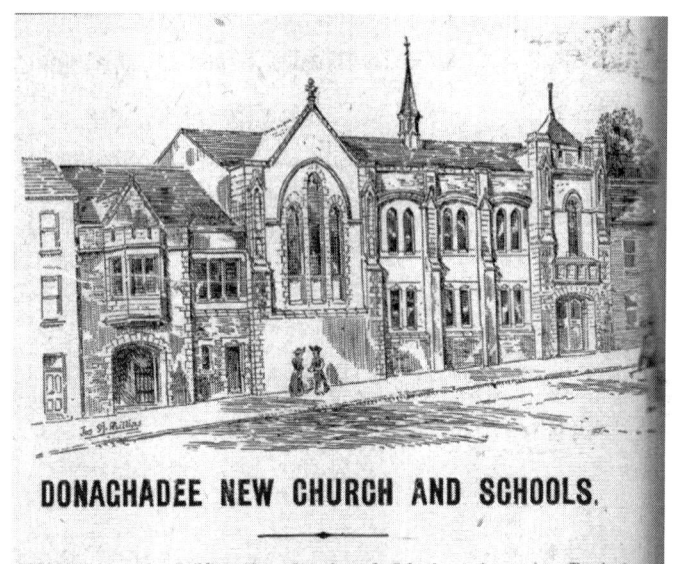

THE Scheme for Building New Church and Schools, and securing Teacher's Residence in this rising sea-side resort, was inaugurated on Wednesday evening week with great enthusiasm. Although the night was most inclement the attendance was good, and the interest in the work unmistakably genuine and hearty. After tea, Rev. Fredk. A. Trotter took the chair, conducting the devotional exercises. Then, in a few appropriate words, he set forth the urgent need for new church premises, and called upon the Congregation to make a united effort then and there to give the scheme a good start.

The appeal in the *Christian Advocate,* 1 June 1906

As the *Christian Advocate* recorded:

> "There is reason to hope that the obstruction in the way of the new church erection at Donaghadee is likely to be surmounted. The necessity of securing a new site at greatly increased expense being obviated by the timely consent of our friend Mr Magowan to relinquish part of the land adjoining the present site for its enlargement. [This will

enable us to build] modern buildings in this central position with all its interesting and historical associations."[81]

However, the money was not available to rebuild the church in accordance with the design which had been published in the *Christian Advocate*. Although the church was extensively refurbished, it was not rebuilt. Instead the inside of it was turned round so that the altar and pulpit were where they are now, instead of on the side away from the road[82]; and the Old Manse[83] was demolished and replaced by the present main entrance and foyer, vestry and pulpit area, all surmounted by a new cupola. The picture overleaf shows the configuration of the church pre-1909, with the pulpit set between tall windows catching sunlight from the South.

The restored church and school were opened with some ceremony in May 1909[84]. The church had been expanded by 50 places, and the church and school together now took in the area formerly covered by the church, the 1822 manse, the 1846

---

[81] *Christian Advocate*, 27 April 1906, p.195

[82] It can be seen from the photograph on p.63 that previously there had been two doors for entry from Moat Street, positioned under the windows at each side.

[83] The original manse dating from around 1822, which had latterly been used as the teacher's residence. The entrance to it can be seen in the photograph on p.84.

[84] Although the restored church bore no resemblance to the artist's impression reproduced on the previous page, that drawing was used again by the *Christian Advocate* in the 1911 article which celebrated the completion of the rebuilding.

THE END OF THE ERA

school and the teacher's residence. A new teacher's residence in Moat Street was purchased in 1908.

The pulpit in its pre-1909 position on the side of the church away from the road

The design of the church attracted comment. It was novel in having the main entrance facing the congregation to make the most of the available space – said to be the only one of its kind in Ireland. Minor changes have been made since, removing some pews and moving the choir and organ down to the ground floor, freeing the space behind the pulpit to be made into a Minister's vestry, but the building is essentially still the same as it was in 1909.

A CHURCH FOR ALL WEATHERS

The cost of the restoration was £2050, or more than £200,000 in today's money, but the church was able to report by the following August that the debt that had been incurred in its construction had been entirely liquidated. The ladies of Belfast had evidently worked their magic again.[85] There is an interesting parallel between the original build in 1812-13 and the rebuilding in 1908-09, in that in both cases women played a leading role in raising the money, and much of that money came, not from Donaghadee itself, but from the commercial heartland of Northern Ireland: in 1812, Lisburn, and in 1908, Belfast.[86]

As a town, Donaghadee had fallen behind Bangor, and behind many towns in Northern Ireland by 1908. It still did not have street lighting, most houses still depended on street pumps for their water supply, and few homes enjoyed main drainage. Donaghadee's first Town Council was appointed in 1908 to begin to tackle these deficiencies.

But Donaghadee Methodist Church was visited and supported by wealthier patrons. The church was regarded as a mission church, and received around 20 per cent of its annual income by way of grant from Home Missions. In all the circumstances the rebuilding can be seen as a bold and ambitious project, which

---

[85] *Christian Advocate*, 26 August 1910, p.397

[86] As in 1812, the fund-raising in 1908 took place against the background of strong economic activity in the industrial heartland of Northern Ireland: Harland and Wolff had just launched *USS Republic, SS Megantic* and *SS Laurentic*, and had three more big liners under construction ready to launch in 1910: *RMS Edinburgh Castle, SS Pakeha* and *RMS Olympic*, elder sister to *Titanic*.

was carried forward quickly and with determination, and it is not surprising that the church depended on outside help to accomplish it.

The church possesses a very fine illuminated address that was presented to the Minister at the time, the Rev James Smyth (1908-1909) at the conclusion of the work. Illustrated with several watercolour scenes of Donaghadee, it speaks of a confident, even an affluent church. The building work, too, had not been skimped: it was all done to a high standard.

Perhaps the support the church received was not so much 'outside' help as it appeared. Many of the leading members of the church at this period gave their principal addresses as being in Belfast: Ballynaveigh or Malone Road, for example. It suggests that a number of Belfast residents had weekend properties in Donaghadee, where they accordingly worshipped on Sundays. Moreover, wherever the planning for the rebuilding was done, it was not in the local quarterly Leaders' Meeting, the minutes of which barely mention the project. It would seem to have been planned and managed mainly by the Property Committee in Belfast.

The spirit of Methodism

Looking at the minutes of the quarterly Leaders' Meetings in the first decade of the twentieth century, one gains an impression of the way Methodist church life goes on, generation by generation, with much the same mundane preoccupations from one year to another. One year there is a deficit in the finances, another year a small surplus. There are grants to be applied for, and supplements to be paid to Ministers' stipends. There are collections to be made for this and that, preachers to be booked for special services, halls to be cleaned and rooms to be repainted. There are heated arguments, the substance of which is rarely recorded, which lead to recriminations and resignations, and new appointments are made. Names often appear which are still present in the congregation a hundred years later.

The main differences between now and a hundred years ago would be the quick rotation of Ministers, who generally stayed for a maximum of three years; the practice of pew rents, which were still in operation – families rented their own pews, where they could sit together, while the other pews that were available to the public were segregated between men and women to prevent any undesirable distractions during worship; and the importance of the Orphans' Fund in the work of the church. The minutes sadly record that the children of Mrs X, or some of them, should now be included in the Orphans' Fund: obviously a matter of critical importance in the days before social security.

A strong emphasis on children comes through the minutes, with much attention paid to the Sunday School, which flourished. What was to become the Wesley Hall still served as a school on weekdays[87], and the schoolmaster, Mr McMillan, who lived across the road in Moat Street, simply carried over his duties into Sunday. Minutes on 8 January 1901 record:

---

[87] As it did until the 1950s.

> "Arranged the children's tea-meeting be held on the 15th February at half past six o'clock p.m. Provision to be made for 120 people. Bloomfield Bakery to supply provisions at not more than 6d (2½p) per head. Mr McMillan to get up a programme for the entertainment of the children and big folk. The prizes to be given to scholars who have attended Sunday School 30 days during the year. Mr McMillan to select prizes."

Methodism was often seen as a severe and somewhat gloomy denomination, but the spirit that breathes through the records is one of service, and even self-sacrifice, but also of much joy, of friendship and fellowship within the congregation and of respect and affection for the Ministers that served the church. It is a tradition that would be immediately recognised by Donaghadee Methodists today.

Conclusion

At the end of the church's first century Donaghadee Methodist Church can be seen basking in the glow of an Edwardian sunset, with Northern Ireland at the peak of its peace and prosperity; with a new manse, said to be one of the finest in Ireland, and church buildings newly enhanced to suit a congregation which included some wealthy members. Some of these were people who did not live in Donaghadee but spent their weekends here in their second homes by the sea.

It is not entirely accidental that this time coincided with the launch and sinking of the Titanic. 1912 marked the end of an era. Society, and especially the middle class way of life dependent on the availability of domestic servants, was about to change for ever.

Already the Great War, which was to be the catalyst of social change, was looming and there was the unhappy sight of a shipload of German arms being smuggled through Donaghadee harbour under cover of darkness to enable Ulster Protestants to resist by threat of force the Government's proposals for Home Rule. With Home Rule blocked by the North, extremists in the South would soon turn to armed rebellion and set in train a succession of Troubles, the last echoes of which have not yet died away.

The fashionable churchgoer in 1905

APPENDICES TO PART ONE

Appendix 1

Extracts from the diary of Mrs Mary Smith[88]

1809

"O that I could love God my Saviour, who has bought me at such an immense price! What an ungrateful hard heart I have to be so insensible of this, and not feel more my lost and miserable state – not even to be afraid of the judgments of God. Sometimes I feel much softened in thinking of my ingratitude, but I never fear Hell! I think, if it was not that I meet in Society with the people of God, and have an interest in their prayers, I would be much worse, and would be forsaken by the Almighty. The enemy has tempted me to think that I have experienced the new birth, because of my being changed from taking delight in worldly amusements as formerly, and now taking pleasure in conversation on religious subjects; and, in place of reading novels, reading the Scriptures and meeting with the servants of God. But I know that I have not peace with God. I do not love Him. I am astonished when I reflect that I am so little cast down – that I am not more earnest in beseeching Him, for Christ's sake, to pardon all my transgressions."

and later

---

[88] Preserved by the Rev John Hill in the memorial of Mrs Smith published in 1858 (Sentinel Press, Londonderry).

"I still see more clearly my lost and miserable state. At the place of worship, while hearing the Word preached, and joining in the prayer meetings, I have shed plentifully the tears of repentance, and I could believe that God was in the midst, and that He would not pass by without blessing me, when I could ask with my whole heart, and I was surprised and grieved when I came away unsatisfied. I took the advice of Mr Baxter, and devoted a particular hour of the day to prayer and meditation. On retiring, 25th March 1809, on meditating on the goodness of the Lord to me since my infant days, and my ingratitude to Him, my reflections threw me into an agony, but, in the hour of my deep distress, I found light and peace."

Hill tells us that:

"Her kind and watchful sister, with whom she retired for prayer, informed us that, while pleading for the promised blessing, her feelings were such that she swooned for a while."

The diary continues:

"I arose and went to my knees, and returned thanks to the Lord for His goodness in thus enabling me to believe that my Saviour died for me, and also for the happiness bestowed in the assurance than my sins were blotted out. I wondered that I could not love Him and praise Him more for what He had done for my soul. Shortly after this day of salvation, I began to doubt that what I felt was not justification. But my Lord and my God did not leave me to cast away my shield. These words were applied to the comfort of my almost desponding heart: "There is therefore now no condemnation to them that are in Christ

APPENDICES TO PART ONE

Jesus" (Rom. viii, 1). I could not take all the comfort afforded by these words till I went to my spiritual friend[89], and, in conversation with her, and in prayer, I was strengthened and my comfort increased."

September, 1810

"Thou Lord hast made me a witness of Thy power to change the heart. Glory be to Thy name, King of heaven and earth; the work is Thine, and Thou hast given me strong confidence and hope that holiness will be perfected, and I shall be kept to the end."

And on 11 March, 1811

"No good work have I to plead, but I have all in my Saviour. He has pardon for all, and for me my Saviour died. O fill me with love divine, and consume all the dross of sin. I long to be purified from all the corruption of my fallen nature, that I may offer unto my God an acceptable sacrifice of praise through Jesus Christ – Glory and praise to my Lord and Saviour, King Emmanuel, through whose infinite merits I am adopted the child of God, and the inheritor of His glorious kingdom."

---

[89] Mrs Dorothea Johnson, of Lisburn

Appendix 2

Extracts from Matthew Lanktree's *Narrative*

The *Biographical Narrative* written by the Rev Dr Lanktree casts a light on the early Methodist Ministry in Donaghadee and the Copeland Islands.

Rev Matthew Lanktree (1770-1849) was appointed to Belfast in 1815 and became Chairman of the Belfast District, which then extended as far as Coleraine. In 1818 he was appointed to the newly established Ards Mission, based in Newtownards, to which Comber was added in 1820. It was in that capacity that he first visited the Copeland Islands. In 1820 Donaghadee and Newtownards became a separate Circuit and the Rev David Waugh became the Minister at Donaghadee.

Lanktree then served in a variety of appointments elsewhere before returning to Donaghadee as Minister in the cholera year of 1832. He had hoped to be on 'light duties' there, with his friend Samuel Harpur, but Harpur became ill soon after he arrived, and he had to shoulder the whole burden of coping with the cholera epidemic. He retired and became Supernumerary in Donaghadee in 1834, continuing to preach there and in Newtownards on alternate Sundays until 1846.

He and his second wife, Catherine, both died of cholera in 1849, his last work having been to minister at the bedside of a poor man who was dying of the disease. They were married in the French Church in Cork, in 1799 and had twelve children together. Lanktree was a man of ability and modesty, with a

APPENDICES TO PART ONE

generous, ecumenical approach: 'a friend of all, and an enemy of none'. He went through some hard times in his Ministry, and suffered many concerns about the health of his wife and children, as well as his own, but always maintained his faith and optimism. His best memorial is the touching Address which his twelve children made to him, inscribed in the Bible they gave him for his birthday in 1828, which expresses with unimpeachable sincerity what a wonderful father they thought he was.

He writes in his *Narrative*:

August 13, 1818

"After an interesting visit to the Copeland Islands, preaching, visiting etc; administered the Lord's Supper to Robert Emberson and friends. It was a most solemn and affecting season, Robert, his wife, parents and children all weeping together. His were the tears that delight, the sighs that waft to heaven.

Sept 11th

"Visited him again and found him rejoicing in hope, the most emaciated living skeleton I ever saw. His family and friends were deeply affected. I addressed them as I thought he would if able. The following Lord's Day I was called to attend his funeral in Donaghadee, and thought to have preached his funeral sermon in our Chapel but the crowd was immense. I therefore preached in the churchyard from Rev XIV 13, trust fruit will follow unto eternal life. Were it only for the grace of

God bestowed upon this man through missionary labours what a glorious prospect does it present in the day of Christ.

Appendix

The Copeland Isle is separated from Donaghadee by a channel two miles in breadth, and maintains 10 families. After the Scotch had settled in this country it was inhabited by Presbyterians who attended divine service regularly in Donaghadee: for which purpose they had a large boat in which they sailed together. It is reported that frequently would their pious Minister and his people watch them whilst toiling to make the shore against wind and tide, and delay the service until joined by these zealous islanders. After that generation passed away the place was uncultivated for many years.

When it again became inhabited it was by a generation that "knew not the God of their fathers". Robert Emberson appeared an exception and mourned over the wickedness which prevailed among his friends and neighbours. He would retire among the rocks to implore the Lord to have mercy on them and to send a Minister to instruct them in the way of Salvation. He who said of Saul of Tarsus "Behold he prayeth" gave this supplicant a gracious intimation that his prayer was granted. Shortly after Mr Hill[90] had been appointed to the Ards Mission

---

[90] Rev John Hill was appointed to the area in 1816, before the Ards Mission was actually established. He worked in Donaghadee and the Copelands and set up Class Meetings also in Cottown, Portavo and Ballyblack. He was appointed Minister in Donaghadee in 1825 and again from 1833 to 1835. He wrote the memorials to the Misses Smith referred to in this history. He tells us there that:

he visited the island and preached to the inhabitants from Mark I,15. Several of them believed his report. Robert received the preacher and his message as from God, became a partaker of pardoning Grace and a witness for the God of his salvation.

A society was soon formed of which he became a Leader. He received much of the mind of Christ and was remarkably qualified to encourage others to follow his blessed Master. He was greatly beloved of the people, the Society prospered under his care and the voice of praise and prayer became general in their habitations.

1819 Aug 12th

"Arrived at Newtownards. Having resumed my regular Ministry I found my colleague an affectionate, lively preacher, much intent on the conversion of sinners, and it pleased God to give us souls for our hire, though our principal work was to edify believers rather than too widely extend our sphere of operation. We had a good and happy year and had the comfort of seeing our Circuit so far matured as to be united to the regular societies around, and thus formed the Donaghadee and Newtownards Circuit.

"By the advice of the late Rev Matthew Lanktree, the Conference, in 1816, appointed the writer [John Hill] as a missionary, to labour in the Ards, Killinchey, and including the places in the neighbourhood of Donaghadee. While labouring in conjunction with the Belfast Ministers, the Lord was pleased to bless the united efforts."

1820

"The South part of our Mission was given to Donaghadee, now formed into a new Circuit for one preacher. Bangor was given off to the Donaghadee Circuit.

1832

"Cholera[91] has now visited our land. Never did I commence a year's labour under such remarkable circumstances. In Donaghadee the cholera raged and carried off some of our people. Pressed by the messenger of death and unknowing who next might be summoned to the cholera house, or the grave, a general concern for eternal life pervaded the community. Our leaders and praying people were at their post and active for God. The prosperous state of the work, however, bore up my spirit and labour, weariness and weakness were sanctified. Two new classes were added to the Donaghadee Society, and in order to accommodate our increased congregations we were obliged to add two new galleries to our chapel."

---

[91] Cholera struck everywhere, not just in Donaghadee, and killed within a few days. It was not realised at that time that it was a water-borne infection, the received wisdom being that it was air-borne, carried by the *miasma* or foul smell from the drains. The organism was too small to be detected in water by the microscopes of the day. For an account of the brilliant and dedicated research work by which the error was corrected and cholera banished almost overnight from the civilised world see Steven Johnson's book *The Ghost Map*, Penguin, 2006 - at the risk of learning rather more than the genteel reader may wish to know about early Victorian sanitary arrangements and the course of the disease.

APPENDICES TO PART ONE

Appendix 3

The Baptismal Register, 1825-1849

The Baptismal records cast a light on the changing character of the Donaghadee congregation in these early years.

These records cover the Ards peninsula right up to Bangor, with some families as far afield as Craigantlet and Dundonald (a couple from Scotland and one from Canada). The various clerks and Ministers who compiled the register were not consistent about the information they recorded. Sometimes they would give the parish and the townland, sometimes just one or the other; sometimes they would record the occupation of the father, but more often (sadly) not.

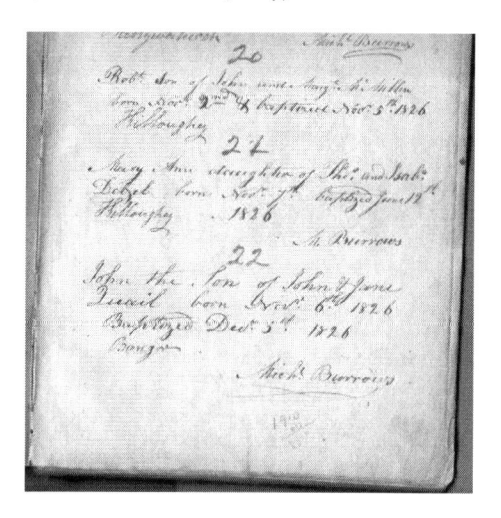

An extract from the Baptismal Roll

Of the occupations recorded, the majority would be labourers, but Newtownards showed a large number of weavers, as one might expect, and Donaghadee an increasing number of boatmen or mariners. Many farming families are represented: there are grocers, butchers, shoemakers, tailors, masons and miners – even a 'wire web manufacturer' from Belfast. There are several coastguards or members of the Preventive Water Guard, as it was known, a lighthouse keeper and a surgeon, Dr Whitley of Newtownards.

Many people in those days would have been uncertain about how to spell their names, and the clerks wrote it as they heard it: 'Beaman' for Beaumont, 'Maginsy' for McGimpsey, and 'Steenson' for Stevenson, for example. A clerk was unfamiliar with the name Benjamin, which appears as 'Bengeman'. The spellings of some localities had not settled down yet, either: Gransha appears as 'Granshugh' or 'Granshaugh', and Ballyeasborough is spelt in three different ways, as is Glastry. Conlig appears as 'Conligo'.

The Christian names given were, to start with at least, very limited in range: John, James, William and Robert for boys, and Mary (or Mary Ann or Mary Jane), Margaret, Jane and Elizabeth for girls, would account for the majority. But with rising prosperity, and with Methodism becoming more respectable and moving up into the middle class, more ambitious names begin to creep in: Charles, Henry and George, Catherine, Harriett and Charlotte, for example. A scholarly Mr McFadden named his unlucky children Theodore and Theodocia. People started giving their children two and even three Christian names, instead of one.

It was a common practice to add family surnames as second Christian names to show family connections, and in this way it can be deduced that several of the Methodist families were interrelated: the Embersons to the Gunnings, the Bullocks to the Lindsays, and the Sharps to the Dalzells. Sometimes people named children in tribute to their Methodist Ministers: 'Samuel Harpur' (twice), 'Matthew Lanktree' and 'Thomas Ballard'.

Particularly moving are some of the little marginal notes that appear in the register. Rev Thomas Ballard records the baptism of his own son in 1841, and then, two years later, notes his death, "My boy is registered in heaven". Jane Anderson Graham was baptized in 1846, but the note reads, "The girl is to be called Jane Anderson and drop the name of Graham, as her father has (if ever married) refused to support her or her mother Ellen Jane Anderson".

About one delivery in a hundred was twins, but the twins do not seem to have fared well. A couple of times the baptism was just the day after birth, which may be taken as a bad sign – on one occasion, actually on the day of birth – and the note reads "baptized same day in consequence of illness". The time interval between birth and baptism generally lengthened during the period covered by the register, perhaps reflecting greater confidence that the children would survive.

A surprising finding is that sometimes parents whose child had died early would have another child and give it the same name.

That would seem strange to us, as though wiping out the memory of the dead child, but it happened more than once in this register.

APPENDICES TO PART ONE

Appendix 4

Ministers at Donaghadee, year by year

1820   David Waugh

Donaghadee & Newtownards
1821-2 Alexander Sturgeon, John Jebb
1823   Alexander Sturgeon, Nathaniel Hobart

Donaghadee
1824   William Keys, William Guard
1825   William Keys, John Hill
1826   Michael Burrows, James Henry
1827   Michael Burrows, John Prusho Hetherington[92]
1828   Thomas Ballard, Robert Beauchamp
1829-30 Thomas Ballard, William Cather
1831   Samuel Harpur, John Waugh
1832   Samuel Harpur, Matthew Lanktree sen
1833   Samuel Harpur, John Hill
1834   John Hill, John Harrington, Matthew Lanktree *Sup*
1835   John Hill, William Hoey, Matthew Lanktree *Sup*
1836   John Nash, William Hoey, Matthew Lanktree *Sup*
1837   John Nash, Robert Black, Matthew Lanktree *Sup*
1838   Thomas Ballard, Robert Black, Samuel Wood, Matthew Lanktree *Sup*
1839   Thomas Ballard, William Brown, Samuel Wood, Matthew Lanktree *Sup*[93], John Wiggins *Sup*

---

[92] Who did not take up appointment but under the direction of the President went to a Circuit in England.

[93] Who resides at Newtownards and preaches there every alternate Sabbath.

1840 Thomas Ballard, James Kennedy, Samuel Wood *Sup*, Matthew Lanktree *Sup*[94]

1841 William Foote, James Donald, Samuel Wood, Matthew Lanktree *Sup*

1842 William Foote, James Tobias, Samuel Wood *Sup*, Matthew Lanktree *Sup* (Newtownards)

1843 James Tobias, Robert A Devers, Matthew Lanktree *Sup* (Newtownards)

1844 James Tobias, George Deery, Matthew Lanktree *Sup* (Newtownards)

1845 William Cather, Wallace McMullen, Matthew Lanktree *Sup* (Newtownards)

1846 William Cather, James Hutchinson

1847 William Cather, John Harrington, James Collier

1848 Thomas Ballard, John Higgins (Newtownards), Samuel McDowell *Sup* (Kirkcubbin)

1849 John Armstrong, John Higgins (Newtownards), Samuel McDowell *Sup* (Kirkcubbin)

1850 John Armstrong, John Higgins (Newtownards), Samuel McDowell *Sup* (Kirkcubbin), Edward Cobain *Sup* (Newtownards)

1851-3 James Tobias, William Hoey 2nd (Newtownards), Samuel McDowell *Sup* (Kirkcubbin)

1854 James Hughes, Benjamin Bayly (Newtownards)

1855 James Hughes, William Lough (Newtownards)

1856 Edward Harpur, William Lough (Newtownards)

1857 William Brown, James C Bass (Newtownards)

1858 William Brown, William Cather (Newtownards), James Olliffe *Sup*, John Hill *Sup*

1859 William Brown, William Cather (Newtownards), James Olliffe *Sup*, John Hill *Sup*

---

[94] As above

APPENDICES TO PART ONE

1860 William Cather (Newtownards), Robert Hazelton, John Hill *Sup*
1861 Henry Price (Newtownards), Robert Hazelton, John Hill S*up*, Samuel Cowdy 1st *Sup* (Newtownards)
1862 Henry Price (Newtownards), Robert Hazelton, John Hill S*up* (Donaghadee), Samuel Cowdy 1st *Sup* (Newtownards)
1863 Henry Price (Newtownards), Frederick Elliott, John Hill *Sup*
1864-5 Jeremiah Wilson (Newtownards), Frederick Elliott, John Hill *Sup*
1866-7 John Hughes (Newtownards), Thomas Cooke, John Hill *Sup*
1868 John Hughes (Newtownards), John Greer, John Hill *Sup*
1869 John Greer, John Wilson (Newtownards), John Hill *Sup*

[*Newtownards and Donaghadee become separate Circuits*]

- 1870 John Greer
- 1871-3 Richard Maxwell
- 1874-6 Oliver McCutcheon
- 1877-9 Robert Jamison
- 1880-2 John Hazelton
- 1883 John Oliver
- 1884-6 Robert M Morrison
- 1887-9 James Wilson
- 1890 Irvine Johnston
- 1891 Irvine Johnston, John W Johnston *Sup*
- 1892 Irvine Johnston
- 1893-5 Samuel Dunlop
- 1896-8 John Magill
- 1899-01 Irvine Johnston
- 1902-4 Robert M Morrison BA
- 1905-7 Frederick Trotter
- 1908 James Smyth LLB
- 1909-11 John W Carrothers MA
- 1912-4 Henry McConnell

PART TWO

Part 2:
The second hundred years
1913 - 2012

The Harbour Lights

The Harbour Lights were formed in 1976. The original members were Brian Mills, Hugh Herron, Charlie Bell and Billy Fergie. The group continued to perform at church and other events until 2011, when Brian Mills sadly passed away.

Chapter 7
The First War

Donaghadee in 1913

The first part of this book described the history of Donaghadee Methodist Church from its foundation in 1813 to 1912. The church building had been renovated and re-modelled in 1909, when the entrance foyer, staircase and tower (or 'cupola') were added, and as we have seen in 1913 it was in a prosperous condition.

Donaghadee was no longer a sea port, as it had been in the first half of the 19th century, but it was a flourishing seaside town. In size it had fallen behind Bangor, because the railway journey from Belfast to Bangor was shorter and more convenient, and Bangor benefitted from property development on a much greater scale, but Donaghadee enjoyed its share of development. Genteel properties for commuters as well as summer residences had sprung up everywhere in walking distance of the railway station: along the Warren Road and the New Road, out along the Millisle Road and a little way up the Killaughey Road. There were several hotels flourishing along the sea front. The population in 1913 was a little over two thousand.

All through the church's second century Donaghadee remained essentially a commuter and holiday town. Commuting by bus and car replaced commuting by train when the railway closed in

THE FIRST WAR

1950, and the hotels closed one by one after the Second World War, but Donaghadee remained an attractive place to live and to holiday. Between the Wars a swimming pool was opened on the front, the golf course was built on the Warren Road and in the summer there were the usual seaside entertainments on the pier.

Harry Allen[95] records that it was a common practice for Donaghadee residents to give up their homes to visitors from Belfast in the holiday season (essentially the week of the twelfth and the week after, but often extending to a month) and retreat into 'back-houses' or sheds behind their houses, thus earning a useful bit of money. That may no longer happen, but its place has been taken by the caravans that now line the coast. There are several large mobile home parks down the coast, whose summer residents provide custom for the Donaghadee traders.

In the 1960s Donaghadee expanded with the building of substantial new estates to accommodate people moving out of sub-standard housing in Belfast; and the building of private housing continued in parallel, extending the boundaries of the town out on all sides, so that by 2001 the population had increased to 6,500. But the town centre has retained much of its character, and, though the streets have been levelled, surfaced and lit in the interval, photographs of it a hundred years ago are still easily recognisable.

---

[95] *Donaghadee, An illustrated history*, published by White Row Press, 2006.

Home Rule

In 1913, at the start of the church's second hundred years, the campaign for Irish Home Rule was at its height. A few Methodists supported Home Rule, believing that the only solution to the country's economic difficulties was to have a locally elected government in Ireland, still as part of the British Empire. But the overwhelming majority were opposed, and the *Christian Advocate* made it clear that that was the official position of the Methodist Church. It was largely a question of Protestant solidarity. There was a fear that Home Rule would extinguish Protestantism in the South of Ireland: "Home Rule means Rome rule" was the slogan.

Methodists organised their own demonstrations against the third Home Rule Bill in 1912. Simultaneous meetings were planned in the Ulster Hall and the Exhibition Hall and special trains were laid on to bring people in from all over Ulster and beyond. In the event a third venue was needed to accommodate the numbers attending. Methodists signed the Covenant against Home Rule in great numbers.

The UVF's gun running into Larne in April 1914 was reported in the *Christian Advocate*, but it omitted to mention the parallel run into Donaghadee. While the *Clyde Valley* docked in Larne on 25 April, the smaller *Innismurray* appeared off the Copeland Islands and berthed at about 5.45am. The UVF had taken over the harbour, with the tacit consent of the authorities, and unloaded a large consignment of arms.

THE FIRST WAR

Many Methodists were by then beginning to have misgivings about the way things were developing, as it was clear that resistance to Home Rule could become very violent. Conference that year passed an uncompromising resolution against Home Rule, but the ambivalence of many members was shown by the fact that it was opposed by 110 delegates, against 143 in favour. However the question of Home Rule was then put on hold as a result of the outbreak of the First World War.

Rev Henry McConnell

In 1913 the Minister here was the Rev Henry McConnell. Born in 1866, he had served mostly in the South of Ireland before being stationed in Donaghadee. He stayed till 1915, when he moved on to Holywood and ended his career there. According to his obituary in the *Christian Advocate*, "His faithfulness as a pastor and preacher and his gift of making and keeping friends made him beloved on all his Circuits".

The church with its new entrance and cupola, as it was redesigned in 1909

The church was prospering at this time, with good attendances both morning and evening. Weekly collections averaged about £2.80, divided roughly equally between morning and evening services, but the totals were augmented by a number of special services[96]. Special services were concentrated in the summer months, when the congregation was swollen with holidaymakers from Belfast. The Annual Appeal on 25 July 1915 raised £18.20, a couple of special sermons by the Rev Wesley Roddie next month raised £20.05, and the Harvest Festival in September raised £7.93 plus £4.32 from the sale of fruits and other produce.

But the weather – good or bad – could influence takings. Disappointing collections of 92p in March 1916 and of 88p in May were blamed respectively on "very mild weather" and on "a very wet day". It shows that even when people were more disciplined about church attendance than perhaps they are today they could still be tempted away or deterred by the weather.

The first Quarterly Meeting of 1913 starts with an obituary 'to be placed on record in the minutes', which may serve as an example to any Church Secretary charged with writing condolences:

> "The Stewards and Leaders of Donaghadee Methodist Church assembled in their Quarterly Meeting desire to place on record their deep sense of the loss this Church

---

[96] These figures need to be multiplied by about 100 to equate to current prices.

has sustained in the death of Mr Martin Wallace, Circuit Steward.

"They remember with pleasure his connection with the Church, his zealous and successful efforts to aid in the erection of our new and beautiful sanctuary, and his very liberal support of Circuit and Connexional Funds. They learn with thankfulness of his peaceful and happy end, and although the messenger of death came suddenly and unexpectedly, he was ready for the call home.

"Respectfully would they present to the bereaved family their sincere sympathy joined with earnest prayer that the Divine Head of the Church may sustain and comfort them in their great sorrow."

The Church Schools in 1913

We have an interesting insight into the working of the Church Schools at this period. They were officially called 'the Moat St. No. 2 National Schools', Principal Mr A. M. M'Millan, and their running was very much integrated with that of the Sunday School, whose Superintendent was also Mr M'Millan[97]. Prizegivings were held for both the National Schools and the

---

[97] In 1916 Mr M'Millan wrote to the Quarterly Board resigning his position as Principal Teacher of the Donaghadee No.2 National School and also as Superintendent of the Sunday School, Secretary of the Quarterly Board and Organiser of the Choir. No reason seems to have been given, and he was politely thanked for his 16 years' service to the Church. Something must have happened.

Sunday School together, when each year "a large company sat down for a splendid tea".

The Church School, about 1919

The Sunday School had 115 names on the roll and an average attendance of 96, with 9 teachers. The Day School had 140 pupils on the roll, with an average attendance of 124, or 87 per cent. This attendance rate "compared most favourably with attendance at the best schools in Ireland", for which the national average attendance rate was 70 per cent. It received uniformly favourable reports from the Inspectors of Schools.

The subjects taught in the Day School were, in 1913, Latin, French, Geometry, Algebra, Experimental Science, shorthand

and typewriting. In 1915 the report adds to that list Bookkeeping, Cookery and Laundry Work. It was obviously a thoroughly practical school as well as an academic one. Rev. McConnell was proud to say that the school taught:

> "not just the 3 R's, but principles of loyalty to the Empire, honour to parents, obedience and respect to those in authority over them, and habits of uprightness, morality and temperance".

Rev Robert Maxwell

Rev McConnell was succeeded in 1915 by the Rev Robert Maxwell, born 1870, who served until 1919. He is reported to have been a forceful evangelistic preacher, but he may not have been the easiest Minister to get on with. There were several resignations of Church Officers on his watch. Nevertheless in 1918 he was warmly thanked for his service and was requested by the Quarterly Meeting to stay on for a fourth year, whereas three years was still the norm at that time.

In June 1915 a clock was presented to the church by Mr Robert Emberson[98] to mark his connection with the church for 80 years. His family had been connected with the church for a full

---

[98] The son of Thomas and Mary Emberson, he had been a sailor. He was born on 28 Dec 1835 and baptised on Jan 4 1836 by the Rev John Hill.

century, since the Rev Matthew Lanktree met his grandfather, also called Robert, on his first visit to the Copeland Islands.

The First World War had three marked effects on the Methodist Church. The first was that, though there was no conscription, a significant number of young men joined up for service in the Armed Forces. The second was the arrival in Ireland of large numbers of recruits to the Army, sent to barracks and camps all over Ireland for training. These often used Methodist halls for recreation, staffed by volunteers from the churches. A huge effort was made by Methodists to look after the troops, which was rewarded in due course by Methodism being given greater recognition in Army, and eventually in Navy, chaplaincy.

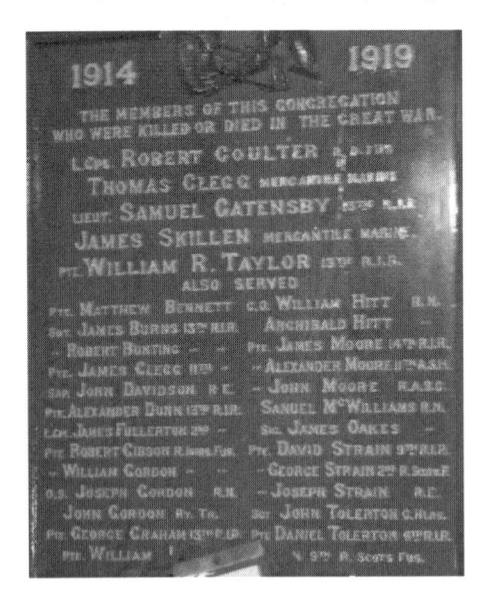

Memorial to those who served in the First World War

THE FIRST WAR

The third consequence was the number of casualties that were suffered. In the Mountpottinger and Newtownards Circuit 360 young men joined up, mainly in the Ulster Division, and 62 of them were killed. Proportionally, Donaghadee's losses were smaller, perhaps because they served in other regiments. Five members of the congregation were killed in action and 25 were wounded. Each Methodist soldier going off to the war was given a little brown cardboard wallet, with printed on it:

The Methodist Church

ON

ACTIVE SERVICE

FOR

GOD AND KING

In it was placed their quarterly ticket of membership. The plaque in the church records their names, first those who were killed and then the others who volunteered to serve in the forces. The plaque was dedicated in June 1920 by Mrs W J Jefferson at a service attended by Old Comrades, the Sea Scouts, a band and bugles and colours[99]. The Last Post was sounded by a Sea Scout bugler and the service ended with the National Anthem.

---

[99] The plaque was originally sited in the porch, and was moved to its present position inside the church in 1938.

Chapter 8
The inter-war years

Rev Robert Teasey, and the first church organ

Rev Maxwell was succeeded in 1919 by Rev Robert Teasey. Born at Caledon in 1873, his father had died when he was three. He left school early and went to work in the Caledon Woolen Mills for seven years. He became an Evangelist in Carrickfergus in 1896 and was called to the Ministry in the following year.

Rev Robert Teasey

He is memorable principally for the attention he gave to church music and the development of the choir. At the end of his time in Donaghadee he organised a Sale of Work to raise the money

THE INTER-WAR YEARS

for an organ, which produced the remarkable sum of £125, or roughly £7,500 in today's money[100].

The Quarterly Meeting of Leaders and Stewards on 30 June 1922 resolved:

> "Mr Clarke proposed, Mr Brown seconded and it was carried unanimously that repairs to the manse be not proceeded with, but that instead an effort be made to introduce an American organ, the money to be raised by putting a box into every Member's house, into which £1 be placed, and to get ten collectors to raise £5 each."

The church was clearly struggling in the immediate post-war period, when there was a recession and unemployment was high[101]. In 1920 it received an annual grant of £50 from Home Missions, which was equivalent to 20 per cent of its total

---

[100] To put that in perspective, the Minister's stipend in 1919 was £15 a month (£900 in today's money). The sexton received £1.33 a month (£80 today), and J Clegg, the organ blower, 22p (£13.50) a month. In 1920 the Minister's stipend was raised to £17, the sexton's remuneration was raised to £1.66 a month and the organ blower's to 25p, but whereas Minister and sexton continued to receive regular pay rises in the years that followed the unfortunate organ blower was held to the same modest level of remuneration until 1937. The organ was pumped by hand until 1943, the organ blower sitting behind a small curtain.

[101] Newtownards was also suffering hard times at this period. It was said that in the town only one person in ten attended church, despite the fact that it boasted four Presbyterian, two Covenanting, two Methodist, one Church of Ireland, one Unitarian and one Roman Catholic church. It also had 70 public houses and 12 pawn shops, "which were no help to the morality of the place". (R L Cole, *History of Methodism in Ireland 1860-1960*)

income, and the church applied for grants from several other sources within Methodism. It was supported by Home Missions until 1947. In 1921 pew rents were producing about £10 per quarter, and they continued to contribute a gradually declining amount each year until 1948, when they were abolished[102].

Despite this, Rev Teasey was able to report that the work was going well:

> "Mr Teasey reported that there were 99 scholars on the Sunday School Roll, being an increase of 15, and that in connection with the Band Of Hope all the Sunday School children had signed the pledge."

Holy Communion was still held only once a quarter, although by that time many Methodist churches had moved to once a month, and Donaghadee Methodist was soon to follow. A Tent Mission was held in Millisle in the summer months, which was the precursor of the outdoor services at Quarry Green.

Thanks to Mr Teasey's efforts the first church organ was eventually purchased. It stood at the back of the choir gallery, as shown in this photograph:

---

[102] However, it is reported that proprietorial rights to certain pews continued long after rents were abolished.

THE INTER-WAR YEARS

The original organ, Harvest Festival c.1923

In the South, a number of Methodists were murdered in the course of the Civil War of 1919-1921 leading up to the founding of the Irish Free State, but Donaghadee was largely untouched by these events. The separate Government of Northern Ireland was established in 1922, with its own Parliament in Stormont and Northern Ireland became the entity we know today – a devolved part of the United Kingdom – but without power sharing until 1998.

Rev William McVitty

Robert Teasey's successor, in 1923, was the Rev William McVitty, who was to have a long association with Donaghadee, returning as a retired Minister in 1939. Born in Clones in 1866, he was to die in Donaghadee just short of his 90th birthday, having served as Minister here from 1923 to 1926 and then as an active Supernumerary from 1939 to his death in 1955. He took over the leadership of the church for six months when the Rev Sam McIntyre died in December 1946.

Rev Wm Presley McVitty

He is still remembered with affection by some church members from this later period, because "his children's talks were so good every Sunday".

A Harvest Festival in 1925 produced collections of £13.70 (£700 in today's money) in the morning, 50p in the afternoon and £25.65 in the evening, making a total of £39.85, and the subsequent sale of produce brought the total to over £50 (£2500 today). Collections were made for special causes, too. £1 was given to 'the Russian Delegation' (presumably counter-revolutionaries), a similar amount to the Egypt General Mission, and in November 1926 83p (a not over-generous £40 in today's money) was collected for the British Legion's Poppy Day appeal.

Rev William E Maguire

The next Minister was Rev William E. Maguire, born at Newtownbutler in 1863 and therefore already 63 at the time of his appointment in 1926. Early in his life he had served in the Open Air Crusade in the midlands of Ireland, but he was already unwell when he was appointed. He died at the Donaghadee manse in January 1928.

It became something of a pattern in the 20th century, though there were significant exceptions, for Ministers to be appointed to Donaghadee towards the end of their active careers, as their last or second last appointment. Donaghadee was regarded by the Stationing Committee as a not-too-demanding station, with its administrative responsibilities simplified by the fact that it was a one-church Circuit.

It is interesting to note how many of the Ministers at this period hailed from the Monaghan/Fermanagh area: Teasey from Caledon, McVitty from Clones, Maguire from Newtownbutler, Bryans again from Clones, Wilson from Cavan, McDonagh from Ballinamallard, no doubt reflecting the strength of Methodism in that region in the second half of the C 19th.

Rev William Bryans

When Rev Maguire died unexpectedly the Rev T E Gibson, at the time Superintendent of the Hamilton Road Church in

Bangor[103], took pastoral charge until Conference could appoint a successor. Born in 1855, he was 72 at the time, and continued in active Ministry to the age of 76, when he was Superintendent at Carlisle Circus.

Rev William Bryans, who took over in 1928, was born at Clones in 1869. He was a Lay Worker with the Belfast City Mission from 1890 to 1895, and served a year as Evangelist at Comber in 1891 before being called to the Ministry in 1895. Of him it is recorded that:

> "He served in some of the most strenuous Circuits of country Methodism. He was indefatigable in the care he gave to the maintenance and renovation of our Trust property, often sharing in the work with his own hands".

Rev Charles Wilson

If Bryans was a practical, 'hands on' Minister, his successor in 1930 was a more academic figure. Rev Charles Wilson was born in Cavan in 1870 and underwent teacher training in Dublin. He became Secretary of the Methodist Orphan Society 1927-1930, and then Treasurer of the Society from 1931-1945. His obituary records that, "A careful student, he sought to lead his hearers into the treasures of reading as well as into the presence and knowledge of God". It was at this time that the Belfast City

---

[103] At that time Donaghadee, like Bangor, was in the Belfast District. It was not until 1988 that it was transferred to the Down District.

THE INTER-WAR YEARS

Mission opened Childhaven, and Charles Wilson, with his [104]interest in working with orphans, established a close relationship with the new home.

Almost the first thing he had to deal with when he was appointed was a row over the auditing of the church's accounts for 1929. The senior Circuit Steward was censured and finally dismissed for having failed to get the accounts audited. This was important becasue the church depended on grants of £50 from Home Missions and £10 from the Laymen's Fund to balance its books. He had to be ordered to surrender all the church books and papers in his possession, and a new Chief Steward was appointed from January 1931.

The next issue was the transfer of the church's Day School to the Down County Regional Education Committee. This was agreed within a few months, as the church considered that satisfactory terms were being offered. The church offered to transfer ownership of the teacher's residence too, but that was declined: instead the Education Committee rented it. In 1937 the Committee sought permission to build a bathroom in it, which suggested that there was no bathroom before, and the church agreed provided no liability fell on the church or on the Methodist Trustees, to whom ownership was then transferred.

---

[104] In 1933, at a time of growing austerity, the grants were reduced to £40 and £8 respectively. The Minister's stipend at that time was £260 p.a.

Another financial irregularity occurred in 1931. The Ministry of Labour asked for £10.88 for Health Insurance for the sexton, which the church had evidently not been paying.

When Charles Wilson left in 1934 the Quarterly Board recorded an elegant tribute to him:

> "From the time he came amongst us his desire has been to serve the Master ... The healthy state of the finances during his Superintendency was proof of his organising skill and ability. As a preacher, while his sermons showed thoughtful preparation and literary skill, the predominant note was evangelical and proved him the faithful and diligent Minister of the Gospel. In the home of sickness and sorrow he was a welcome visitor and his kindly words and practical sympathy were gratefully received."

Childhaven and the Belfast City Mission

The Rev Crawford Johnson established the Belfast Central Mission in 1889. It was first located in the Sandy Row Methodist Church, then in a tent and in a circus hall, until finally, in 1895, it acquired its own premises, Grosvenor Hall, between Grosvenor Road and Fingall Street. The Hall was rebuilt in 1927.

The Mission had an impressive record of working with the destitute, and in particular with the young 'Street Arabs' of the city. In 1928 Mr and Mrs Turtle gifted Templepatrick House and its grounds to the Mission, and in June 1930 Childhaven

THE INTER-WAR YEARS

Children's Home was opened, together with a holiday home on the lower slope of the Childhaven site. Mr John Young was appointed manager.

The years that followed were the Hungry Thirties, and Mr Young reported frequently to the Mission Committee on the malnutrition and "frightening physical condition" of the children. In most summers, according to Eric Gallagher's history of the Mission, a total of at least 700 children had holidays lasting two weeks; in 1934 the total was 730, and in 1937 50 adults were also holiday guests. The task of organising this with all due care was stupendous.

The church provided regular Sunday evening services at Childhaven for some years.

Rev Francis Scott Maguire

In 1934 Rev Charles Wilson was succeeded by the Rev Francis Scott Maguire. Born in Dublin in 1885, he was the son of Rev William Maguire, but no relation to the Rev William E. Maguire mentioned above. He came to Donaghadee from Newtownards and went on to be Superintendent at Osborne Park in Belfast.

He would appear to have had independent means, because when, on his arrival, £80 was spent on smartening up the manse and installing electricity, he claimed only £15 and paid for the rest himself.

Rev Scott Maguire

The weekly pattern of church meetings at that time was as follows:

> Sunday Services: 11.30 and 7pm. Sunday School: 2.45pm
> Gospel Service in Childhaven, June to September: 8.15pm
> Monday: Quarterly Meeting at 8pm
> Tuesday: 'Help Heavenward' Meeting at 8.15pm
> Wednesday: Junior Christian Endeavour 7.15pm, Girls' League 8.15pm, Choir 9.15pm
> Thursday: Senior Christian Endeavour 8.15pm
> Friday: Second Friday in the month, Ballyhay Gospel Service 8pm.

Christian Endeavour had become an important part of the church's work by this date. Started in America in 1882 as the Young People's Society of Christian Endeavour, it soon spread to Ireland, with the first church adopting it being Agnes St Presbyterian in 1889. Agnes St was followed within a couple of

THE INTER-WAR YEARS

years by Knock Methodist, and by 1895 it had been adopted by Conference as the official youth movement of Irish Methodism. Its strength and appeal was that it combined worship with study, missionary interest, social responsibility and recreation.

In 1936 the Quarterly Board decided that the church needed comprehensive repainting, and they asked the Education Committee if they would like to paint the school at the same time and share the cost of the contract proportionally. In the event the Board found that it could only afford to paint the exterior of the church, and the inside was left until 1938, when the church ladies undertook to raise the money for that part of the project.

In 1939 the Girls' League was thanked for the gift of a Communion Table.

The Church School in the 1930s

One member recalls the Church School in the 1930s. Her father, brothers and sisters all attended the school. Originally all fitted in the one room, the Wesley Hall as it now is, except that there was no stage. Then more children came as evacuees during the War, and School was divided, upstairs and downstairs. The Head, Mr A Wilkinson, taught upstairs, while Miss Moore was in charge downstairs.

Mr Wilkinson is remembered as " a great leader", and "a Local Preacher held in the highest esteem as a Christian and as a teacher"[105], while Miss Moore is remembered as "authoritarian but lovely". Other teachers were Miss Mullen, Mrs Cowan, Mrs Lithgow and Mr Billy Collett. The children got bottles of milk and hot chelsea buns each day. They wore no uniform in those days, and brought lunch with them in their schoolbags. There was a lot of discipline, and the cane was used when necessary.

---

[105] In 1937 he took over as Secretary to the Quarterly Board when Mr James Wells moved to Lisburn to take up the post of Principal of a school there.

Chapter 9
War and recovery

Rev Robert McDonagh

Rev Robert McDonagh took over from Rev Maguire in 1939. Born at Ballinamallard in 1894 he was to die in 1946. He is remembered as "a tall, good-looking man", who liked to cycle out to the farms with a shotgun to shoot rabbits. During the War his wife Edith became Conductor of the Donaghadee Male Voice Choir, and the Methodist Manse provided accommodation for rehearsals (evidently the choir was not as numerous then as it was to become).

Rev Robert McDonagh

Rev McDonagh was extremely popular, and whereas it was the usual practice for churches to wait until the third year before inviting a Minister to stay on for a fourth and then a fifth year, the church took the unusal step of asking him after just one year if he would stay for the full five years (which was at that time the maximum).

The Second World War

The Second World War had a much greater impact on Northern Ireland than the First. Shortages in supplies of food, fuel and other goods were much greater, and because the North was the only part of Ireland available to the Allies there was a large concentration of American and British troops here for the purposes of training and defence. Royal Engineers from Scotland were billeted in boarding houses on Shore Street and the Air-Sea Rescue Service commandeered the building known as Ocean Drive. A temporary airfield was built out at Killaughey.

Methodist halls again played their part in accommodating the troops for recreation, staffed by volunteers from the churches. The greatest impact, however, was the blitz of Belfast, which, although it was short in duration (April and May 1941), inflicted terrible damage and loss of life. Relations with the South were strained during the War, and it became difficult for Methodist Ministers to cross the border, but that was by comparison a minor inconvenience.

The War years were terrible in many respects, but they are recalled as having been a time of bustling activity, and not all bad. History relates that several local girls found husbands in visiting servicemen (British or American) and small boys recall having been given cans of pineapple chunks by GIs from their stores behind the pier.

The war had a direct impact on the church. As early as September 1939 the blackout meant that a Guest Tea had to be cancelled. In 1940 the church tried to bring evangelists over from Cliff College but there were no sailings from England. No special mission was possible during the blackout, and the church held a musical evening instead of a congregational social. In January 1941 it was agreed that a Mr Silverwood could come over from Cliff in late summer. He found it hard to get a permit for crossing, but after applying to the Passport Office he was told that a permit would be granted but not issued until 10 days before the sailing[106].

In 1941 the pay of the organ blower was raised to £1 per quarter (sexton £1.50 per month), but he was not to enjoy that enhanced level of remuneration for long. In 1942 the church decided to purchase an electric organ blower at a cost of £47, but since there was a war on the work could not be done until 1943. In the event, including installation it cost £81.67 – "a heavy item", as the minutes record.

In 1943 the Home Missions Secretary suggested that it was time Donaghadee became a non-dependent Circuit. The church leaders noted that "under war conditions givings to the church were much above normal" but felt that "the time was not

---

[106] As late in the War as 1944 the President of the British Conference was unable to cross the Irish Sea to preside at the Irish Conference.

opportune for such a sacrifice". They offered the Secretary a donation of £10 instead. Eventually, however, in 1947 the church gave up its annual grant from Home Missions.

Also in 1943 the church decided to approach Mr Hopes (a local landowner) to see if he would sell the room adjacent to the church which later became the Old Choir Room[107]. Mr Hopes initially wanted £600, which was considered to be too much, but after negotiation he agreed to let it to the church for 50 years at £13 a year, which the trustees regarded as "splendid terms". The room became known as the Church Parlour.

The opening of the Church Parlour was accompanied by a service for the dedication of new Civil Defence colours. "From the church the congregation moved to the entrance of the new building", reported the *Christian Advocate*, omitting to say that it was only next door. Friends of the church gave pictures, chairs, a table and a clock to furnish it. It was regularly used for meetings of the Quarterly Board and many other meetings[108] up to 1994.

When Mr McDonagh left, church membership stood at 198, which was the highest total for 46 years, and it continued to advance under his successor.

---

[107] Having fallen into disrepair it was handed back to the landlord in 2011.

[108] In 1946 the Donaghadee Male Voice Choir paid £4 for use of the Parlour, which was added to the Organ Fund. They used the Parlour on Monday evenings until 1948, when it came to be required for Christian Endeavour meetings.

WAR AND RECOVERY

Rev Samuel McIntyre

Rev Samuel McIntyre, who succeeded Rev McDonagh in 1944, was born at Stewartstown, Tyrone, in 1874, and was therefore already 70 on his appointment. He was to die in office in December 1946.

He was, according to his obituary, "a careful student of Holy Scripture, and his preaching was expository and evangelistic". He is remembered for having had an Austin 7 car, and for being "very strait-laced". One member recalls him asking, "What are you doing at a dance class?"

His unmarried daughter Dorothy stayed on in Donaghadee and was still teaching Sunday School here in 1959. Members remember that she used to come to church on a bike and leave it in the foyer.

During the War the manse lost its iron railings to salvage and got a low brick wall instead. It was not possible to replace the railings until 1950. When Rev McIntyre moved in to the manse new curtains and carpets were urgently required, but it was impossible to obtain the material for curtains[109], and carpets were prohibitively expensive. They wanted to make a new glass fronted notice board for outside the church, but the wood was not available.

---

[109] Even in 1952 it proved hard to obtain curtain material for the manse.

Despite his dour reputation, Samuel McIntyre was a progressive Minister, and he carried the church forward effectively in his short tenure. By 1945 membership had reached 207, and the next year 214, together with 94 junior members.

Soon after taking over he invited the young people to assemble in the Church Parlour to ask them what would be the most suitable evening to hold a young people's meeting, and also what nature of a meeting would most appeal to the young.

Rev Samuel McIntyre

In 1946 he appointed a Committee to take forward work with young people. There was a poor response initially, so the Committee decided to focus on the 9-14 year olds. At the first eeting only 12 turned up, but the numbers soon reached 100[110].

---

[110] The young people quickly decided that the harmonium they were using was out of date, and in 1947 they bought a new piano for £50.

But by that time he was seriously ill. In October he announced that he had decided he would retire next year, but he died in December. The church had granted him £50 towards the cost of the expensive treatment he was receiving – no Health Service in those days[111]. He was remembered for his "fine qualities, earnestness and high Christian character".

The Church Leaders hesitated to ask the 80 year old Supernumerary, Rev William McVitty, to stand in for Mr McIntyre; but he did so, and acquitted himself with distinction until Rev Sam Baxter arrived next July.

Rev Samuel Baxter

With the Rev Samuel Baxter, who was appointed here in 1947, we enter the period of which a number of members of the current Donaghadee congregation have a clear and lively memory. Baxter, who had an MA and was granted a DD in1968, was a man of energy and ability. Born in 1908, he was younger than most Ministers at Donaghadee have been[112].

---

[111] The nature of his illness is not recorded, so probably cancer, which was never spoken about in those days.

[112] He started life as an apprentice druggist and became a Lay Evangelist at the Crumlin Road in 1927, entering the Ministry next year at the age of 20, when he was assigned to the Londonderry City Mission.

Rev Samuel Baxter

He had a strong impact on the life of the church, particularly with his work among young people. It is reported that he would buttonhole young people in the street and ask them if they were saved. He is said to have had the gallery packed with 15, 16 and 17 year olds. At one time Christian Endeavour, meeting on Monday nights, had 30 members, and the Tennis Club in summer 20 members. Members recall that the church was so full at times that people filled up the aisles with chairs.

The "Sunshine Corner" is remembered as having been a wonderful meeting for young people. The church bought a projector for £30 for their use. The Minister's Bible Class for young men got off to a strong start. In 1948 there were 120 on the Sunday School roll, with average attendance of 90, and 12 teachers. The Girls' League had 26 members, and Christian Endeavour 28 (of whom 24 were full members).

WAR AND RECOVERY

In 1947 women members[113] attended the Quarterly Board for the first time in about 50 years.

In 1948 the Council gave permission for the church to use Quarry Green for services on Sunday afternoons. The church ordered a supply of hymn sheets, a loudspeaker (£25), seating, and a supply of handbills to be distributed by Christian Endeavour. In 1952 Gordon Campbell proposed building a platform and stand at Quarry Green to hold forms, chairs etc and provide shelter for the speaker, using good second-hand timber and volunteer labour. Mrs Stone, the landowner, had no objection, but pointed out that the church might be liable for rates on it. Perhaps deterred by that thought, no permanent structure was ever built.

The second church organ

In 1945 Rev McIntyre had started a fund to purchase a new organ, and for the next five years it was the major focus of fundraising in the church. The cost was estimated at £1750, equivalent to six years' stipend for the Minister. By the end of 1947 the Organ Fund had reached £445, and by 1948 £520. At that point Glastry Methodist Church asked if Donaghadee would let them have the old organ. The Quarterly Board asked for £550, and not a penny less than £500. Glastry went elsewhere.

---

[113] Miss A L Kerr, Miss Adams, Mrs Roberts, Mrs J G Campbell, Mrs W Campbell.

The firm building the new organ subsequently offered £300, and the church eventually sold the old organ to Omagh for £350. One way or another, almost all the funds were assembled by 1949, and the organ was ordered. Its completion was delayed, however, because the builders were not able to obtain some parts.

In 1950 there were special services on 12, 13 and 14 August, when the new pipe organ was dedicated and two new memorial windows were unveiled. The windows[114], which were erected by the Ardill[115] family in memory of the late Mrs Violet Ardill, had already been dedicated on 30 July in a service with Mr McClean[116] as organist.

For the ceremony in August the President of Conference and the Minister of High Street Presbyterian attended, and the guest preacher (who seems to have spent some time in Donaghadee) was the Rev John Broadbelt, who had been Principal of Cliff College 1932-48. For good measure a further ceremony of opening and dedication of the pipe organ was held on Saturday

---

[114] The windows are on the South side of the choir gallery, or what is now called the sanctuary area.

[115] Capt Austin Ardill was a leading Unionist politician. Elected to the Stormont Parliament in 1945, he was Chairman of the Loyalist Association in 1971 and Deputy Leader of *Vanguard* in 1972.

[116] Mr McClean was appointed choirmaster and organist in 1944, on the death of Mr Bertie Lynas.

23 September, when the organ was opened by Miss J Adams and the guest organist was Mr T S Turner.

Although the church had assembled most of the money to pay for the organ it had not allowed for heavy expenditure on preparations for its installation and alterations to the choir gallery and pulpit, which put pressure on the church's finances for a time.

In 1951 an Evening Service was broadcast by the BBC Northern Ireland Service.

In 1952 the Rev Baxter left Donaghadee with permission to visit the United States (a privilege from which Irish Methodist Ministers rarely returned) but he did come back. He had a short period as Superintendent of the Belfast City Mission, which suited his evangelistic preaching style. He ended his career as Superintendent at Carrickfergus in 1979 and died in August 1988.

The Church School, about 1950

Chapter 10
Salad days

Rev Samuel Crawford

In 1950 the church invited the Rev James Wisheart[117] to succeed Samuel Baxter in 1952, and that invitation was confirmed in April 1952. But Conference decided otherwise.

The Rev Samuel Crawford (1906-1989) succeeded Rev Baxter in 1952. Before entering the Ministry he had been a drapery store assistant in Derry and a Lay Evangelist at Swanlinbar in 1928. He was to return to Donaghadee as a Supernumerary in 1972 and 1973.

His obituary in the *Christian Advocate* said:

> "He had two outstanding gifts: his pastoral work and his ability to organise. This made him a creative leader in the church and in the community".

The church prospered under his leadership, with membership reaching 250 adults and 135 juniors in 1954. He is said to have held three weddings in one August.

---

[117] Rev Wisheart had been appointed the first Superintendent of Evangelism in 1945 and served as such till 1952, the first of three Ministers who held that position up to 1962. The choice is indicative of the mood of the church at that time.

Rev Crawford was popular for his work with young people. Members recall that there would regularly be a sing-along at the manse, when there would be twenty bikes outside. His wife was an enthusiastic helper.

Rev Samuel Crawford

He was an innovator in many ways. On Coronation Day in 1953 there were two television sets provided in the church so that everyone could follow the occasion. He started a class for Local Preachers, with seven members. He introduced the idea of 'Children's Church', which meant that younger children could go out of Morning Service and have their own worship[118]. He also introduced the practice of celebrating the offering with a dedicatory prayer while the collectors stood at the Communion

---

[118] Sunday School was held in the afternoon and entirely separate from that. The age limit for Children's Church appears originally to have been 5, but it was raised to 7 in 1958. It came to be called 'Junior Church' in 1970, perhaps reflecting a further relaxation in the age limit.

rail. And in 1954 film services began in the church on Saturday evenings.

The main issue he faced was the handing back of the school building by the Education Committee in 1953. In July 1953 the new Donaghadee Primary School was ready, and children were transferred into it from all the separate schools which had up till then run in various buildings in the town. There was much disappointment that Mr Wilkinson, the Head of the church's school, was not made Principal of the new Primary School. He was widely regarded as the best candidate.

The church asked for £800 to cover depreciation and repairs to the school building, but its bid was unsuccessful. It now had to decide what to do with the building and with the teacher's residence across the road in Moat Street. It decided to sell the residence and to integrate the school with the church, turning it into the Wesley Hall and creating access from the one building to the other both at ground and at first floor level. The church bought 50 steel frame chairs at 63p each, and later that year another 71 chairs at 65p.

In 1957 the sexton's wage was increased from £42 to £60 p.a. to reflect the extra work involved in looking after the Hall. Church organisations were asked to contribute to the cost of maintaining it. It was let out to visiting Sunday Schools and to the Girls' Life Brigade in the holidays. The church would have liked to make further improvements to the property – for example, installing a proper kitchen - but the money was not available.

The pattern of work in the church at this time is illustrated by the following typical pulpit notice for 5 December 1954:

1. Sacrament of the Lord's Supper at the close of this Service.
2. Sunday School 2.45pm
3. Bible Class 3pm in the Vestry
4. Meeting for prayer 6.20pm in the Vestry
5. Service this evening at 7pm Rev S J Crawford
6. Monday: Junior CE (Christian Endeavour) at 6.45pm
7. Monday: Young People's Senior CE at 8pm
8. Tuesday: mid-week Service at 8pm
9. Wednesday: Girls' League at 8pm
10. Thursday: Meeting for prayer and fellowship at 8pm
11. Thursday: Choir practice at 9pm
12. Saturday: Film Service 7.30, music by the Saturday Choir
13. Services next Sunday 11.30 and 7pm Rev SJ Crawford
14. Retiring offerings at both services next Sunday for the Xmas Poor Fund

The church's programme included regular bus trips to Belfast to watch evangelical (or otherwise improving) films and to listen to evangelists in person. The Sunday School too enjoyed an annual outing. In July 1955 it was to Bellevue: "Buses leave church at 2.15pm, Parents' tickets 30p including tea[119]. Scholars please come for tickets on Wednesday in the Church Parlour at 8pm".

Christian Endeavour had a more adventurous outing the same month: "Buses for the CE trip to Rothesay leave church on Wednesday morning at 6.45am". How they got to Rothesay and

---

[119] About £7.50 in today's money.

when they returned is unknown: Larne to Ardrossan and then a paddle steamer from Ardrossan to Rothesay, perhaps? Or direct via Campbeltown? A fantastic outing, however they did it!

Rev Crawford with members of Christian Endeavour

The same month there was a Garden Party held at Childhaven at 3.30pm on Saturday in aid of the church's Repair Fund. Tickets were 13p including afternoon tea. Relations with Childhaven were close in this period, with the children and young people not only attending services but also being invited to the church for tea. In 1957 the church organised a public collection for Grosvenor Hall and Childhaven, and the volunteers from the church raised £75 (or about £1800 in today's money) on a Saturday in the streets of Donaghadee.

Meanwhile during the summer the church was participating in regular outdoor services, which had been re-started by the Rev

Sam Baxter. There was a weekly service at Quarry Green[120] on Sundays at 3.30pm, and for a week every summer there were open air services on the Parade at 8pm each evening, all other church meetings being cancelled for that week. The Rev Kyle rounded Sundays off with an Epilogue in church at 10pm. There were often soloists performing at the outdoor services, and they featured also at some regular church services in this period.

In May 1956 there was a musical performance by the Junior CE "assisted by guest artistes", tickets 8p each, on 9 June a Sunday School excursion to the Copeland Islands, and on 10 June a parade of Apprentice Boys at the Evening Service. In May 1958 there was to be a joint Junior and Senior CE outing to Templepatrick: "If weather unfavourable, games in Wesley Hall. Meet in church at 7.15pm." Tennis and bowls continued to be popular social activities.

It is worth giving a flavour of the richness of church life at this period, because there is a sense in which it represented a high water mark for Donaghadee Methodist Church. Membership numbers peaked[121] at 254 in 1955 and the range of activities –

---

[120] These services were usually accompanied by a five-piece band, which marched out from the church with a banner. Sometimes they were joined by the Salvation Army Band or Ballyholme Brass Band.

[121] Coincidentally Methodism in Ireland peaked in 1955 with a membership of 67,000; 60,000 of them being in the North and 7,000 in the South. The number of Ministers in active service was to fall from 168 in 1963 to 147 in 1971, indicative of the way the climate was becoming less favourable.

SALAD DAYS

especially for young people – was at its height in the 1950s. Ten years later the Rev Frank Bolster[122] attempted to give a fresh impetus to the church's work with children and young people, but by then the world was changing and some of the church's traditional activities were beginning to look old-fashioned. In 1971 the Young People's Christian Endeavour was to close "because of the lack of teenagers in the congregation".

An open air service at Quarry Green

This was to become a constant worry over the remaining years of the century. The church's premises were looking increasingly

---

[122] See page 164

dated, and there had been cultural changes in the 1960s with which the church struggled to come to terms.

Rev Thomas Kyle

The Rev Thomas Kyle (1909-1995) had succeeded Rev Samuel Crawford in 1955. He entered the Ministry from Portadown at the age of 19, and was described by the *Christian Advocate* as "a wise counsellor and patient pastor, who won the confidence of many by his quality of steadfastness".

Rev Thomas Kyle

Kyle was not the church's first choice: in February 1955 its preferred candidates were, in order, the Revs S D Ferguson, Richard Greenwood and John England. The church then asked Rev Crawford to stay on. But Conference again took no notice.

Rev Crawford and his wife had found the furniture in the manse riddled with woodworm, and had managed to replace some of it, but when Rev and Mrs Kyle moved in it was evident that extensive further work was needed. By 1957 £968 had been spent on the manse and £236 on the church, and the church's liabilities stood at £1074. Even after receiving £811 from the sale of the teacher's residence that year the church still needed to appeal for £300 to clear its debts.

Rev Kyle recognised that the school buildings were not ideally suited as church halls, and invited an architect to draw up plans for a new church hall. In the financial circumstances, however, these plans, which would have cost between £3750 and £5800, were never going to be realised, and after the architect had left the meeting the Trustees concluded that they were "beyond our requirements".

On 6 May 1956 Rev Kyle dedicated a silver rose bowl in memory of Mr William Campbell, who had died the previous year[123].

---

[123] Mr Campbell had been a Circuit Steward, as were his sons Gordon and William. His wife Jean was the local Red Cross co-ordinator at the time of the Princess Victoria disaster in 1953 (when the passenger ferry from Stranraer to Larne sank off Donaghadee with the loss of around 250 lives). He was a driving force behind the purchase of the new organ and helped in the establishment of the Summer Open Air Work at Quarry Green and the Saturday night film services. Jean Campbell was a Class Leader, Sunday School teacher and "hospitable hostess". Gordon Campbell's niece recalls attending Christian Endeavour and endless church sales, "one big sale after another", for which her mother would make things and bake. Members of the Campbell family are commemorated in two of the stained glass windows on the Moat St side of the church, which were installed in the 1990s.

In 1957 the Methodist Conference invited churches to answer two questions about the acceptability of women in Ministry. To their credit Donaghadee's leaders voted, by a small majority, that:

> 1. they had no objection to a woman fulfilling the office of a Methodist Minister; and

> 2. a woman Minister would be accepted on this Circuit.

It was, however, another 50 years before that was to come to pass. The first woman Minister in Irish Methodism was not appointed until nineteen years later, in 1976.

The choir, meanwhile, was less progressive on the issue of gender equality. They minuted the Quarterly Meeting somewhat ambivalently:

> "We wish that Miss Adams be appointed organist, but if this is not possible we would like a male organist as we feel the present arrangements are not satisfactory."

Alas, Miss Adams[124] was not well enough to take up the role.

---

[124] Miss Adams had a remarkable career of service to the church, filling practically every office open to her at one time or another. Apart from playing the organ (which she had done since the 1930s) she taught Sunday School and worked tirelessly for Overseas Missions. She helped Rev Kyle to produce his church history in 1959, and despite her deteriorating health continued to appear in one capacity or another for many more years.

SALAD DAYS

In 1958 a new company of the Boys' Brigade was formed in the church and held its first meeting on 18 April under the leadership of Mr Robinson.

In 1959 the Rev Kyle published a short history of Donaghadee Methodist Church, which had attached to it a convenient summary of all the church organisations at that time and the principal families connected with the church. It records that the members of the Circuit Quarterly Meeting in 1959 were[125]:

Rev Thomas Kyle
Mr E Davidson
Mr C Bell
Mr W Hall
Mr H McCaughan
Mr J G Campbell
Mr S Brown
Mr S Bell
Miss M Bennett (Secretary of Supernumerary Ministers' Fund)
Miss M Brown
Mrs J Laughlin

---

[125] Under John Wesley Circuits had been governed by Superintendents who took all decisions under his delegated authority. It was only after his death that lay members were given a significant share of the responsibility. In the middle of the C19th the Quarterly Meeting, comprising Ministers, Lay Preachers, Stewards and Trustees, became the governing body of the Circuit. It is interesting to note the size of the Quarterly Meeting in 1959. Up till the Second World War the Quarterly Meeting had generally numbered ten or fewer. It continued to grow over the remainder of the century until it reached over 40 in Donaghadee in the 1990s (and as many as 200 in the Newtownabbey Mission). At that time the Methodist Church in Ireland undertook a review of its management structures, and in 2006 Donaghadee's Quarterly Meeting was replaced by a Church Council of around 13-15 members.

Mrs H McCaughan
Mrs J G Campbell
Miss D McIntyre (Sunday School Treasurer)
Mrs S Weir
Miss E McCracken
Mr F Kerr (Freewill Offering Steward)
Mr T Menary
Mrs E Lynas (Secretary of Quarterly Board)
Mrs D McAuley (Freewill Offering Steward)
Mr W Bennett (Society Steward)
Mr J McCracken (Circuit Steward and Sunday School Superintendent)
Mr J Cairns (Circuit Steward)
Mr D McAuley (Society Steward)
Miss J Adams (Secretary of Overseas Missions and Sunday School)
Mrs T J Kyle (Representative of the Women's Department)[126]

Under the heading of the Choir, three organists are listed: Miss Adams, Mrs Bennett and Mrs Kyle. The other organisations listed are:

> Sunday School
> Young Worshippers' League
> Women's Fellowship
> Young People's Society of Christian Endeavour
> Men's Fellowship
> Young Women's Missionary Fellowship
> Junior Christian Endeavour Society
> Saturday Night Film Service

---

[126] The Women's Auxiliary was set up in 1906 to encourage support for overseas missions. It had a junior branch called the Girls' League. In 1928 the Women's Auxiliary became the Women's Department of the Irish Auxiliary to the Methodist Missions Department, generally called just 'the Women's Department'. In 1972 it joined up with other, smaller Methodist women's organisations to become the Methodist Women's Association (MWA).

SALAD DAYS

Life Boys
Youth Club

In addition to a regular pattern of weekly meetings, Summer Open Air Services were held in July and August at Quarry Green on Sundays at 3.30pm, and in the first complete week after the July 12th week at Lemon's Wharf at 8pm each night.

Rev Tom Kyle at Quarry Green with the Salvation Army Band

Rev Robert Good

The search for Rev Kyle's successor was even less sucessful than the previous two. In 1958 the church invited Rev S J C Lindsay and Rev S Callaghan, neither of whom was able to accept. They then invited Rev Wesley Gray, who also declined. Finally they submitted the following list of candidates in order of preference: Rev E Shaw, Rev D J Allen, Rev J V Currie, Rev V Silcock, Rev

Hugh Allen and Rev G W Bryson. But Conference once again decided otherwise.

The Rev Robert (Bob) Good, who took over from Rev Kyle in 1960, was born in 1892 (and therefore 68 at the time of his appointment). His father, Peter Good, had been an RIC Constable and farmer in County Cork. He entered the Ministry from Armagh at the age of 24[127]. He was President of Conference in 1958.

Rev Robert Good

---

[127] A few years later, in 1920, he won a national prize for an essay on 'Spiritual regeneration as the basis of national reconstruction [in the aftermath of the World War]', which reflected a strong concern for the socal gospel but a consciousness that material improvement would not be enough in itself.

In February 1962 he dedicated a Communion Table, Kneelers and Communion Rail presented by Gordon, Cecil and William Campbell in memory of their parents, Mr and Mrs William Campbell. A vote of thanks was moved to Mr Edward Davidson and Mr Albert Lee for their work preparing and polishing the communion rail (which had in fact been made by Mr Davidson). At the same time an organ hymn book was presented by Miss J Adams in memory of her mother.

In July and August 1963 Bob Good had an exchange of pulpit with the Rev Bailey from Bellaire, Ohio. The Bailey family was warmly welcomed to Donaghadee and surprised many of the congregation by providing a wooden cross for display in the church. The family was able to visit again in 2011.

Bob Good's obituary says of him,

> "His genius for friendship, gift of humour and sincerity won him the affection of young and old alike. He gave himself unsparingly to the work of the Church to which he owed so much".

When he died in 1983 the journalist Alf McCreary wrote a generous article about him in the *Belfast Telegraph* for 17 June 1983, entitled 'The Good Life'.

Chapter 11
The climate changes

Rev Frank Bolster

In 1965 the Rev Frank Bolster was appointed to Donaghadee. Born Herbert Lancelot Frank Bolster in Belfast in 1923, his parents were a bus driver and a milliner. Converted at 19, he became a Local Preacher at 24, working at the time as an aircraft engineer with Short and Harlands. At the end of the War in 1945 he went to Cliff College. In 1954 he married Margaret (Peggy), a Civil Servant, and immediately took her off for three years in the Leeward Islands, serving in Montserrat, Antigua and Curacao.

Still in his early 40s when he came to Donaghadee, he displayed great energy. He immediately moved to improve the church's finances, and in May 1966 special gift day services were held in an effort to clear the debt on the recently installed boiler. The subject for a morning service sermon was "Paying our way". The church made a determined effort to persuade members to covenant their donations: the high rate of income tax in those days meant that for every pound donated the church could reclaim 70p from the Revenue[128].

---

[128] A Christian Stewardship campaign had started in 1962, and by 1976 42 members were covenanting their donations.

THE CLIMATE CHANGES

Rev Frank Bolster

Rev Bolster developed a plan for his Ministry, which was structured as a series of quasi-military operations. His strategy was reported in an extensive article in the Christian Evangelist for 22 February 1968, under the headline "New Patterns in Donaghadee". *Operation Evangel* comprised *Operation Check-up* ("We will ask ourselves questions about the Church's task today"), *Operation Hearthstone* (a series of three lectures on the Home and Family from the Christian point of view), *Operation Know-how* (a series of study groups) and *Operation Outreach* (a series of special services conducted by the Rev Wesley Gray).

He held open meetings to attract interest, for example one in *The Plaice* on Tuesday 7 November 1967 (admittance including refreshments 2/6d). *The Plaice,* a coffee bar for young people which was his creation, was in the upstairs Minor Hall, which was decorated with fishing nets, oars etc. It was destroyed in the 1976 fire.

In June 1966 the church was able to announce that Christian Endeavour now comprised three societies: Junior, Senior and a new Young People's Society under the leadership of Eddie Davidson and Albert Wright. The young people were promised rambles and a sausage sizzle on the Copelands.

The Girls' Brigade Company was founded in 1967 with Mrs Dorothy Wright as its first Captain, and in 1968 it held its first display in the Orange Hall at 7.45pm on 3 May. Rev Bolster presided, and Mrs Bolster presented the awards. The Chief Guest was Miss J T McAlees, Assistant Matron at the Ulster Hospital in Dundonald.

The organist and choirmaster when Frank Bolster arrived was Mr Adrian Holmes, who also edited the monthly Newsletter. He was soon succeeded by Mrs Taylor. When, in 1968, she indicated her wish to retire she was succeeded by Mr Robert Watson, who has held that position with distinction ever since.

Rev Bolster also set about building extensions to the Wesley Hall, comprising a new kitchen, toilets and offices. These were opened on 13 December 1969 by Mr John Brown of Bangor and the Rev Eric Gallagher, the Church's representative on the Education Board. In his address Rev Bolster recalled that the School had been built in 1846, rebuilt in 1908 and then handed back by the Education Authority in 1953.

For years, he said, the church had been dreaming of having a modern kitchen and other facilities. There was an acute need for them, with 50 girls on the roll of the GB, with four officers, and the Boys Brigade with 21 boys on the roll and six officers.

THE CLIMATE CHANGES

In addition there was Christian Endeavour, the Women's Fellowship and Women's Department and "a very active bowling club", which had recently acquired two new, full-length mats.

The cost of the extensions was £8000. Regrettably there was confusion about the instructions to the Methodist Trustees (who held the investments for the church) and the church's investments were sold at the worst possible time, which made the cost more burdensome than it needed to have been.

Shortly after, the manse at 7 Millisle Road, known as 'Epworth', was sold for £5000 and 64 Millisle Road (soon re-christened 'Epworth' in its turn) was purchased as a cheaper replacement[129]. The new manse was spacious and well located, but it was cold in winter, difficult to maintain and lacked some amenities. It soon needed a new roof, and a further £6,500 was spent on necessary improvements in 1991. In 2008 the Church Council decided that the cost of heating and maintaining it was too great, and it was sold and the following year a new, more functional manse was purchased in Breckenridge.

Rev Frank Bolster was a great organiser. He produced a Blue Calendar for the church every six months showing the forthcoming events for the church organisations for the next six

---

[129] 64 Millisle Road cost £3950. 7 Millisle Road had been the manse since 1893, and was built on the site of a previous manse ('Wesley Lodge') built by Mrs Mary Smith in 1836.

months. In 1970 he set up, or revived, a strong Youth Leaders' Meeting, comprising:

The Minister, Rev Frank Bolster
The Secretary of Youth Leaders, Robert Watson
Representative of the Quarterly Board, William Fergie
Representative of the Leaders' Board
Superintendent of the Sunday School, Mr A Wright
Secretary of the Sunday School, Miss D Preshaw
Cradle Roll Secretary, Mrs Cedric Armstrong
Junior Church, Miss Sadie Brown
Junior CE, Mrs C Bell
Young Persons CE, Mr Norman Bennett
Leader of Primary Sunday School, Mrs J S Brown
Girls' Brigade, Mrs A Wright and Miss V Foster
Boys' Brigade, Mr Johnstone Baxter
Junior Boys' Brigade, Mrs E Davidson
JMA Secretary, Mrs Lynas
Bible Class, Stuart Kennedy
Plus co-opted members, Mr Roy Stewart, Mrs Gourley and Mrs McCaughan.

This powerful Committee met regularly and took progress reports from each organisation. But despite all the energy Frank Bolster put into this work, it was becoming more difficult to interest young people in church activities: the climate was changing.

In Britain and much of Europe the 1960s had seen a rise of scepticism and a falling away from religion among young people after they left primary school. That was not so much the problem in Northern Ireland, where Christian beliefs were so much a part of the respective national identities.

THE CLIMATE CHANGES

But at a practical level, more parents now had cars, so it was easier to take children to other activities. Children could meet up with their friends elsewhere, and were no longer tied to the church. People – especially at weekends - did things as a family or with friends, rather than as a church. This made it harder for the church to maintain regular participation in its activities.

It was in Frank Bolster's time that the churches in Donaghadee first started to share regularly in Holy Week Services, as they do to this day. In 1972 Rev Bolster launched yet another initiative called 'Contact 72', with a Bible Week from March 19th to 26th led by the Rev Hamilton Skillen of Lurgan on the theme that "Life is relationship".

The Troubles

Frank Bolster's Ministry saw the start of the most recent Troubles in Northern Ireland. At the start of the conflict, with the civil rights marches in 1968, Conference adopted an even-handed approach. It had welcomed the joint initiative in 1965 between Prime Minister Terence O'Neill and Taoiseach Sean Lemass to bring about greater cooperation between North and South, and now it supported a programme of reforms designed to create political and social justice between Protestants and Catholics.

But as the conflict moved towards violence in 1969 the Methodist Church, like all the mainstream churches, tended to withdraw into its shell, and the few courageous individuals, like the Rev Eric Gallagher, who persisted in calling for mutual respect and cooperation with the Catholic Church were rewarded with abuse and ostracism from their own side. As Cooney says[130], although not many joined the paramilitaries, Methodists were not of one mind: views ranged from the extreme [militant] to the liberal[131].

This made it hard for Conference to speak on the issue, but when it did make statements they were carefully worded and constructive. Methodism came out consistently on the side of justice, and for negotiation, not confrontation.

The Troubles made it harder for the Methodist Church in Ireland to function across the North/South border. Already in 1969 Christian Endeavour was finding that it was no longer possible to attend rallies and conventions in the South. In 1971 the offices of the Irish Christian Advocate and the associated highly successful bookshop at Epworth House in Belfast were destroyed by an IRA bomb, and the *Irish Christian Advocate* went out of existence. It was replaced by the *Methodist Newsletter* in 1973.

Several churches in Belfast closed during the Troubles as their congregations moved to less dangerous areas: Falls Road,

---

[130] Cooney, p.111

[131] As an illustration of the pressure within Methodism, a group of churches broke away in 1970 to form the Irish Methodist Revival Movement, which became the Fellowship of Independent Methodist Churches in 1973. Their reason for seceding was their concern about the Methodist Church's involvement in ecumenical activities through its membership of the Irish Council of Churches.

THE CLIMATE CHANGES

Primitive St, Carlisle Memorial, Ligoniel, Lynn Memorial, Ormeau Road and Crumlin Road; and others suffered temporary disruptions.

As the conflict went on, a few churchmen continued to play a critical role in maintaining links with both the Catholic Church and the IRA – often better links with the IRA than the Catholic Church was able to make, inhibited as it was by its overriding concern not to be identified with the paramilitaries. Eric Gallagher received and passed on a message from the IRA in 1971 looking for a way out of the violence even at that early date; and (with Stanley Worrall of Methody) he was one of those who met with the IRA at Feakle in 1974. But all these initiatives fell on stony ground, given the mood of Unionism at the time.

Later in the conflict the Methodist Church did better than most other churches in voicing the case for justice and reconciliation and passing positive resolutions at Conference. It licensed selected Ministers to act as intermediaries in the interests of peace, without any obligation to report back to Conference on their activities. Other churches largely disowned their ecumenical 'mavericks' and (in the opinion of many) did less than they could and should have done to promote the just settlement that was necessary for a lasting peace. Sadly, the Methodist Church was too small a component of Irish Protestantism to have much influence on the course of the conflict.

Donaghadee itself was not greatly touched by the Troubles – there were two bomb attacks, neither of which caused serious injuries – but the many local people who had friends and relatives in the security forces and all those who had cause to travel into Belfast regularly were profoundly affected. There was a 'Policeman's Service' in the church in 1971 to mark the church's concern for the forces of the Law, and several more police services were held over the next thirty years, reflecting the importance of the police in the local community and the church's concern for them at this time of grave danger.

Donaghadee as a town was growing, with new families moving into the estates, and economically it was faring better than many parts of the Province. There was housebuilding going on and the carpet factory, built by Cyril Lord in 1958, was still a major employer. Cyril Lord went bankrupt in 1968, but the factory struggled on under a succession of owners until its final closure in 2005.

Rev Wesley Gray

Frank Bolster served in Donaghadee for eight years before handing over to Rev Wesley Gray in 1973. Rev Gray likewise served for eight years. Born in 1925, he was the son of an RUC Sergeant and became a Local Preacher at the age of 17.

Wesley Gray was known as an evangelist: his strength lay in preaching and outreach work, rather than in church administration. This was a time when a large number of families were being moved out of Belfast and relocated in Donaghadee, and Wesley Gray was active in going out into the new estates and showing himself willing to listen to anyone's problems. He

THE CLIMATE CHANGES

put in long hours around the church, attending all the activities that were going on.

Rev Wesley Gray[132]

In 1975 there was an inspection of the church buildings, which found that there was a need for substantial repairs. The roof timbers, including the tower, were badly affected by woodworm and wet rot, and the advice was that the work must be done urgently or the church would have to close. The cost of the work necessary was estimated at £26,000 – an enormous sum for the church in those days[133].

---

[132] The badges are Christian Endeavour (Ireland).

[133] Equivalent to about £250,000 today.

Rev Wesley Gray sent round a circular to every member of the congregation explaining that the situation was critical and they would have to meet the cost without counting on assistance from elsewhere. He asked for separate supplementary weekly contributions from each family. He hoped that from about 200 families the church would be able to raise an extra £5,000 a year and thereby pay off the debt in five to seven years. That was the origin of the practice of asking members to contribute regularly both to the general church account and to the Building Fund. The repair work started in early 1976, but it was soon to be overtaken by events.

The Great Fire

On 23 June 1976, at about 2.45pm, a fire broke out in the roof of the church. The contractors who were repairing the roof employed two firms of subcontractors, who were both on site at the same time. One firm was using a blowlamp to seal strips of roofing felt on top of the roof, while the other was using a highly flammable liquid to treat the roof timbers below for woodworm and rot. A piece of felt caught fire and fell into the roof space, where it ignited the vapour from the inflammable liquid, and the whole roof instantly went up in flames.

Despite the prompt attendance of the fire brigade, the damage was extensive. The church roof was gone, as was the roof and contents of the Minor Hall; the organ was ruined, and a whole catalogue of furnishings and other items were destroyed. So intense was the blaze that the surveyor's report said:

> "The majority of the steel members have been twisted and distorted beyond repair, while the timber roof members and the ceiling have been completely destroyed. The two corners of the building towards the rear of the church have been pushed out by a few inches due to the expansion of the steelwork. The timber and slated roof over the adjoining hall has also been destroyed completely."

The cost of repair was estimated to be over £50,000[134] in addition to almost £20,000 which the church owed to the contractors for the work they had done up to the date of the fire. And to make matters worse it emerged that the church had been under-insured, so that Methodist Insurance would only pay 40 per cent of any claim, i.e. £20,000 out of the £50,000 required[135]. It was clear that the church would need to pursue the contractors and their insurers for damages on the grounds of negligence.

The proceedings in the High Court were complicated because there were three firms involved, each of which tried to blame the others, and lasted nearly six years, consuming an enormous amount of the time of the church officers involved. Until the damages were received in 1983 the church's annual financial

---

[134] Nearly half a million pounds at today's prices.

[135] The 1970s were a period of very rapid inflation, which exceeded 20 per cent a year in 1976, so it is perhaps not surprising that the insured value had been allowed to fall below the current valuation of the property.

reports speak of it 'groaning under the weight of debt'. The Church Council had to ask its bank for an overdraft of £40,000 as well as being granted an emergency loan of £25,000 by central Methodism and receiving a welcome grant of £8000 from the Joseph Rank Benevolent Trust.

Despite the uncertainty about where the money was going to come from, the church immediately commissioned the rebuilding work, and for the next year, while the work was going on, it met in what is now the Baptist Chapel[136] on Millisle Road. Services moved back into the church in May 1977, when one of the first (on 29 May) was to include an act of thanksgiving for the Silver Jubilee of HM the Queen.

Other church organisations met in a variety of locations:

- The Girls' Brigade and Christian Endeavour used the Moat Lawn Hall

- The Youth Club used the British Legion Hall

- Children's Church used the Scout Hall

- The MWA used the Parish Sunday School Hall

---

[136] The church was formerly the Admiral Leslie Free School for Girls, built in 1872. Mrs Martha Leslie of Rosebank House endowed it so that 30 of the neediest young girls of the town could receive a free education. Other girls paid a penny a week to attend. When it ceased to be used as a school the building was taken over by the Church of Ireland as a Parish Hall, and it was they who kindly allowed the Methodists to use it.

- The Choir used Shore St Presbyterian Church Hall
- Harvest Services were held at Donaghadee Primary School.

Ideally, the destruction caused by the fire would have been the chance to rebuild the church from scratch, but as we have seen the money was scarcely available to repair it, and a major reconstruction was never an option.

Rev Wilfred Agnew

Rev Wilfred Agnew, who was appointed to Donaghadee in 1981, was born in Dublin in 1921. The son of a Senior Staff Officer in the Northern Ireland Civil Service, he too joined the Civil Service and became a Senior Clerk. He became a Local Preacher at the age of 20, but did not become a Minister in full connexion until 1950.

In 1952 he married Jean at Knock Methodist Church, and she was to become his right hand in the Ministry, combining leadership in women's activities with a structured programme of hospitality at the Manse.

He inherited a church which was struggling with debt and with ongoing property problems, and it was he who first actively began to think about the possibility of moving the church to a new site. When the compensation for the fire damage was received and the debts were settled he found that he still had to call on the congregation for increased giving, and the spectre of further property expense was always hanging over him.

Wilfred was a lifelong student, and some members found him a bit intellectual and distant, but he is remembered by all with affection and respect. He was extremely systematic about visiting members of the congregation. He came back to Donaghadee and served with distinction as a Supernumerary from 1991 to his death in 2010, at which time his loss was keenly felt.

Rev Wilfred Agnew

On the coast just south of Millisle stands a large white house, which is now the NI Prison Service College. In the 1970s and 80s it was a Borstal, or training school for young offenders. Its Superintendent, Ernie Whittington, was a Circuit Steward at Donaghadee. Boys from the Borstal attended services at several churches, five or six of them coming to the Methodist Church attended by a couple of guards. It is said that they caused no trouble there beyond scratching 'UDA' on a pew, but they were a problem for residents in the Millisle area, because they regularly escaped and stole from houses. One day when the van that brought them drew up outside the church the five young men ran off and hid in the woods up at High Trees, but they were quickly apprehended and corporal punishment was administered.

In 1987 Wilfred (already a year over retirement age) moved to Glastry Church. He was still officially Superintendent of Donaghadee Methodist Church and continued to administer Holy Communion here, but most of the time he was away from Donaghadee, so there was in effect an interregnum for a year.

For that year the church enjoyed the Lay Ministry of a young man called Robert Bowen, from Cornwall, who was a Circuit Evangelist. Mr and Mrs Agnew vacated the manse, and he took their place there. It was a popular and successful appointment. Being in his 20s himself, Robbie is remembered particularly for his work with young people, though he discharged the full range of pastoral duties while he was here. He wore shorts in all weathers, and rode around the town and countryside on a bicycle. After ordination he went on to display great courage as a missionary in West Africa.

Rev George Campbell

Wilfred Agnew's successor in 1988 was the Rev George Campbell. He was born at Enniskillen in 1943, the son of a farmer, and was educated at the Technical Day School, from which he went on to work as a Civil Servant in the Department of Agriculture. He went from Donaghadee to Dundonald, which was to be his last pastoral charge.

With his appointment, Donaghadee moved from the Belfast District to the Down District. This did not make a great difference, because Donaghadee continued to be a single church Circuit somewhat isolated from its neighbouring societies, but it explains why contact with the North Down churches is less than might be expected from their geographical proximity.

Rev George Campbell

Rev Campbell was to devote much of his energy to the search for a new site for the church. As we have seen, he was not the first Minister to have realised that the church buildings were neither adequate for present needs nor suitable for the longer term. Rev Tom Kyle had been thinking of a new church hall as early as 1955, and in 1966 Rev Frank Bolster had his eye on the garden of the neighbouring No.8 Moat Street to provide more space for a possible new church hall. He wrote:

> "It might be possible to erect the hall on the high ground with a more useful width, say up to 30 feet".

But 8 Moat St was not available, and without it they had only 20 feet for a hall, which was not enough. He had to settle for an extension to the Wesley Hall, with a new kitchen and toilets.

In 1975 there was the adverse report on the property which led to the costly and ill-fated repairs of 1976. Then there was the fire, and more expense on repairing a property which everyone recognised was not ideal and would require continuing money spent on it. Wilfred Agnew in 1984 was faced with the need to spend more money on repairing the church roof and its parapet facing Moat Street, and the survey at that time pointed to a potential cost of some £70,000[137] to bring the premises fully up to standard. He started to think about a radical rebuilding, but was advised that it would cost about £42 - £46 per square foot[138] and since the money was plainly not available he did not proceed.

---

[137] About £200,000 at today's prices. It has to be borne in mind that the church building essentially dates from 1849. The restoration and reconfiguration of the church in 1909 left the basic church building intact.

[138] About £1200 to £1300 per square metre at today's prices.

As soon as George Campbell arrived in 1988 he set the ball rolling by writing to his Catholic colleague in Bangor and asking if there would be any possibility of the church purchasing one and a half to two acres of land adjacent to St Anne's Chapel. The request was referred to the Diocesan Office, and Bishop Cahal Daly replied in very cordial terms saying that he would wish to be able to assist the Methodist Church but was advised that it would not be wise for the Catholic Church to relinquish so much of the vacant St Anne's site. He asked the Rev Campbell whether a smaller area might be acceptable. Rev Campbell in turn took advice from his architect, who said that one and a half acres was really the minimum necessary, so he wrote with regret to Bishop Daly declining his offer.

His attention next turned to the site of the petrol station at the other end of Moat Street, which was up for sale. He quickly realised that the site on its own would not be large enough, so he wrote to Mrs Stone, the local landowner at the Manor House, to ask if she would be willing to sell an additional parcel of land behind it. Unfortunately the petrol station was sold before the church was able to put in an offer.

In September 1989 Rev Campbell asked Mrs Stone, if the church could buy one and a half to two acres of greenfield site in the High Bangor Road/New Road area. Mrs Stone explained that the land was being sold to a developer, but she put him in touch with the firm, which subsequently (in 1992) offered the church one and a half acres at the corner of what is now Breckenridge and the High Bangor Road for £140,000. That offer was declined partly on the grounds of expense and partly because there was a feeling in Council that the church should aim to stay in the town if at all possible: Breckenridge (not yet developed) was regarded as being too far away from the centre of gravity of the congregation.

The other site available in 1989 was the old gas works site behind the pier head, but the Quarterly Meeting dismissed it on the grounds that the location was not attractive.

In February 1990 there was another condition report on the premises, followed by a Commission visitation in November, which confirmed that, though the building was basically structurally sound, rather than spending more money on the present buildings the church would do better to build on a new site. The cost of bringing the existing buildings up to standard was put at £100,000.

At this stage approximately £1000 a quarter was being spent on minor maintenance, and there was also heavy ongoing expenditure on the manse.

Meanwhile, in May 1989, a local estate agent had offered the church No 8 Moat Street for £40,000, an offer which the Quarterly Board declined as being too expensive - and in any case they were looking to move elsewhere. By August 1992 the price had come down, as the Lawson property bubble collapsed, and it was available for about £20,000. By then, the option of moving to a new site had receded, and the church eventually purchased No.8 for £25,000 in February 1993.

In 1994 the builder's yard behind the church site, with an entrance on to Church Lane, came on the market at a price of £40,000. The disused site was regarded as a hazard, because children were scrambling over the rough ground and the rusty sheds. Rev Lee Glenny acted swiftly on a resolution of the Leaders' Meeting, writing to the Secretary of the Property Board and asking for urgent permission to purchase it together with the ends of two adjacent gardens which would complement the recently acquired site of 8 Moat Street. By the end of 1994, therefore, the church had acquired the whole site of No 8, parts of several adjacent gardens and the current car park, and for the first time it enjoyed access to the rear of the premises.

Youth work in Donaghadee

In 1991 Youth for Christ Northern Ireland were in touch with Rev George Campbell about the possibility of a YfC 'Summerserve' team, comprising young volunteers from a variety of countries, visiting Donaghadee. This youth mission took place in 1992, and Youth for Christ decided to follow it up with a conference to consider the possibility of setting up a Drop In Centre for young people in the town. A couple of meetings were held that autumn[139] in the Dunallen Hotel, which led to the Drop In Centre being established in 1993.

Donaghadee Methodist Church was (and remains) a supporter of the Drop In Centre, but it continued to look for ways of

---

[139] John Caldwell drew up a paper identifying and assessing various options for the location of the Centre.

providing more for young people within the church itself. As we have seen, as long ago as 1970 the church had been conscious of a shortage of young people in the congregation. D L Cooney notes that:

> "The 1970s were years when young people began to move away from the structured organisations. They disliked much of the planning, and felt restricted by the traditional youth activities. The new development of that decade was the Youth Club ... where activity was much more casual."[140]

A survey by the evangelical consultant Wilson Doran[141] in 1983 again highlighted the problem, saying that the church was failing to reach out to young people. In recent years the Sunday School has been doing doing well enough, and there have been highly successful Holiday Bible Clubs for primary age children in the Summer holidays, but once children become teenagers it has been hard to retain them.

Twice in recent years the church has recruited a part-time Youth and Family Worker to try to tackle this problem, but it has continued to prove difficult to involve the older young people.

---

[140] Cooney, p.178.

[141] Wilson Doran ran the Lay Witness programme, which he had helped to set up with a small team in 1975. The programme continues to this day.

Rev David Houston

Rev David Houston was appointed to Donaghadee in 1993. Born in 1940, the son of an accountant, he was educated at Magee College in Londonderry. He is remembered as always having been frail, although when he was in the pulpit he seemed to gain strength which carried him through.

Sadly he served only a year before he was given permission to be without pastoral charge on grounds of ill health. Had he stayed he proposed to set up a Church Youth Council to consult about the future property needs of the church and what young people would be looking for from their church, thus bringing together the themes of church redevelopment and a focus on youth which have been so salient in the last 20 years.

Rev David Houston

Chapter 12
The once and future church

Rev Lee Glenny

The Rev J Brownlee (Lee) Glenny was appointed in 1994. Born in 1945, the son of an RUC Sergeant, he taught at the Methodist College. He entered Edgehill College in 1983 and was then appointed to the South Derry Mission in 1986, at which point he became a Minister in full connexion. He has several publications to his name.

Rev Dr Brownlee Glenny

An evangelical with a keen interest in outreach to young people, he devoted much energy to the idea of a church redevelopment. He set out a strategy for development based on three phases:

1. Purchasing additional ground to the rear of the church to provide sufficient space for future redevelopment.

2. Redevelopment of church hall to provide adequate room for a variety of youth organisations, MWA and other community activities.

3. Redevelopment or extension and improvement of existing church premises.

The church's architect was invited to work on the plan and identified the following options:

1. A new hall at the rear, linked by a central concourse, with 8 Moat St converted into three good, usable rooms.

2. As above, but also enlarging the church to take in part of the Wesley Hall.

3. Build a new church behind the present one, and convert the existing church into halls and meeting rooms.

4. Sell all the property facing Moat Street and rebuild behind.

5. Flatten the whole site and rebuild.

Despite Lee Glenny's best efforts the development plan never got beyond the first phase of his strategy. The land was acquired, and in 1995 the church obtained outline planning permission for a new church hall in the car park, the creation of a 3m wide pedestrian access from Moat Street to the carpark and a vehicular right of way entrance from Church Lane. But that was as far as it went. The money was simply not there.

Lee Glenny had two other concerns about the church property, which in the event took priority. The first was the need to refurbish the kitchen, which was done in 1999. The second, which he passed to his successor, Robert Russell, was the restricted space at the front of the church. "The choir area is very limited", he wrote, "as is room around the Communion table. Youth participation, drama, etc. presents physical difficulties and constraints".

In 1996 the Quarterly Board considered a proposal to remove the front pew in church, especially to give more room for funerals, but it proved more complicated (and more controversial) than at first thought and the idea was dropped. Another suggestion that the pews should be upholstered was, however, adopted.

In 1997 Childhaven asked if the top floor of No.8 could be converted into flats for some of its workers, but the church decided that it would be uneconomic. Access to the top floor was restricted and it would have been expensive to create an adequate fire exit. For that reason the rooms at the top of No.8 have continued to be used only as storerooms.

Property expenses continued, with significant expenditure on electrical work in 1997 and the urgent need to refurbish the kitchen and the toilets, which was planned in 1998 and executed in 1999. There was a constant stream of work needing to be done, and the Property and Finance Committee always had a heavy agenda.

Property apart, Rev Lee Glenny's main focus was evangelism. He was a strong supporter of the Youth for Christ initiative, and invited Lay Witnesses to visit to reinvigorate the church's work. He sought for ways to attract young people by, for example, introducing new styles of worship incorporating more modern music. 'Praise' became a feature of the church's services. He also started, in 1995, a creche led by Hilda Butler to help more young families attend worship. Despite these efforts the church's numbers declined during his time: a visiting Commission in 2000 noted that membership had fallen to 131, from 147 ten years earlier.

The Methodist Church in Ireland was at this time trying to get its thinking in good order for the new millennium. In 1999 a 'Clearing our Vision' exercise was launched, which led in 2000 to the production of a Mission Statement and a list of aims and objectives for the Church over the next five years[142]. Though not novel or groundbreaking, these aims and the values that underpinned them had a distinct influence on the thinking of Donaghadee Methodist over the succeeding years.

---

[142] The headings under which the objectives were grouped were:

>Prayer
>Worship/Fellowship
>Discipleship
>Ministry
>Caring
>Evangelism/Outreach

THE ONCE AND FUTURE CHURCH

Rev Robert Russell

Rev Robert Russell succeeded Lee Glenny in 2001. Born in Lurgan in 1944, the son of a baker, he worked as a textile designer before entering the Ministry. He served as a missionary in the Caribbean, and was Secretary of the Methodist Missionary Society (Ireland) when he was appointed. He retained a strong interest in overseas work.

Robert Russell realised that something needed to be done about the property, and that there was a dilemma about whether to spend money on maintenance and refurbishment or to focus on a new build, whenever it could be afforded. His view, expressed to the Quarterly Board in October 2001, was that the choice needed to be examined as a policy or mission issue, not just as a matter of economics. The church, he said, needed a strong base from which to reach out into the community.

Lee Glenny had fired the congregation up to expect major redevelopment and had encouraged contributions to a development fund, but as the prospect of rebuilding faded those contributions were tending to dry up, and the chances of obtaining external finance had not increased. The finances of the church were in good enough shape for the purposes of current spending, but could not support a major investment project. Robert Russell therefore concentrated on making the inside of the church more attractive and more usable.

Rev Robert Russell

Robert brought a strong interest in the church's work with children and young people. The flyer reproduced overleaf shows the range of activities for young people he introduced in his first full year, 2002.

Chatterbox, for Mums and Toddlers on Tuesday mornings, was his idea, and he was a strong supporter of the proposal for a Christian counselling service, eventually called 'Connect' which started in 2003, a little later than the flyer had indicated.

Under the direction of Joan Bell, 'Connect' became an important part of the church's commitment to the local community. Since opening in 2003 it has worked with more than 250 clients. Recently it had seven trained counsellors and five members of an administration team. It works closely with the local Mental Health Teams and GPs and has developed a system of initial assessment and counselling practice which aims to meet the needs of clients. It is run by a Management Board which includes representatives of other churches, and it operates on an inter-denominational basis.

'Connect' Christian Counselling
was opened by Lady Sylvia Hermon MP (second left) on 31 May 2003, pictured here with Maeve Lennie, Joan Bell, Margaret Douglas and Kathleen Russell

Although it offers distinctively Christian counselling it does not discriminate in the provision of its services on religious or any other grounds. It holds a Coffee Morning in the Manor House each year to raise funds. This has become an inter-church community event, with local primary schools providing musical entertainment.

A CHURCH FOR ALL WEATHERS

DONAGHADEE METHODIST CHURCH

We welcome people of all ages to a warm,
friendly and caring church

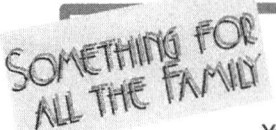

SOMETHING FOR ALL THE FAMILY

Sunday

Worship Services
11.30am and 7.00pm

YoYo's - 10.00am (Young Ones)

All at 11.30am:
Nursery (for sleepers & crawlers)
Teddy Bear Club (for walkers & talkers)
Sunday Club (for primaries)

Kids & Teens

GB Explorers - Tuesdays 6.00pm
GB Company Section - Tuesdays 7.15pm

'The Gig' (young ones) Fridays fortnightly

Beginning September
'Connect' (Kid's club for 5-11yrs)

To be confirmed
Ju Jitsu (martial arts for primaries)

Community Service

'CHATTERBOX'
Mums / Carers &
Toddlers
opening September
2002

Free Counselling &
Advice Centre
Opening October, 2002

Luncheon Club (Seniors)
2nd Tuesday 12.30pm

Aerobics &
Weightwatchers
meet on Mondays

Adults

Teaching & Fellowship - Wednesdays 7.30pm.
Men's Fellowship - Fridays 7.30pm (monthly)
M.W.A. for women - Mondays 8pm (fortnightly)
and Wednesdays 2.30pm (fortnightly)
House groups (monthly)
'Rooted in Christ' - nurture group Wednesdays
Bowling Club - Thursdays 7.30pm

Minister Robert Russell
Tel / Fax 91 88 35 34
E Mail r.russell0@talk21.com

COME AND DISCOVER EXCITING OPPORTUNITIES FOR WORSHIP, TEACHING,
ACTIVITIES, COUNSELLING, ADVICE AND GOOD TIMES TOGETHER. WE WOULD LOVE
TO SHARE OUR RESOURCES AND EXPERIENCE WITH YOU.

A flyer advertising activities for children and families, 2002

Despite Robert Russell's enthusiasm for work with children, Sunday School numbers continued to fall in 2002 to the point where the Superintendent had to report that a separate school in the afternoon was no longer viable. Accordingly, from September 2002 the Sunday School was amalgamated with Junior Church and took place concurrently with the morning Service. The following year the leader of YoYo (the Young Ones) meeting before Morning Worship at 10am reported that YoYo *and* church was proving too much for its members, and it was agreed that instead the first part of every Morning Service would be directed towards the younger members of the congregation.

There was an important development in 2002 when the Methodist Church in Ireland signed its Covenant with the Church of Ireland[143]. This declaration of mutual respect and recognition was followed in 2011 by practical proposals for the sharing of Ministry, the benefits of which will surely be felt over the coming years.

Rev Lee Glenny had already noted that the front of the church did not lend itself to participation by children and others in acts of worship, and was also a hindrance at funerals. In 2002 Robert Russell resolved that changes should be made, removing the front and side pews, creating a platform at the front, moving the organ down under the balcony to one side and walling off the rear of the choir gallery to form a new vestry.

---

[143] The signatories were the Rev Winston Graham, President of the Methodist Conference, and Archbishop Robin Eames, Primate of All Ireland.

This suggestion proved controversial, and representations were made to the Quarterly Meeting that it would be costly and the money could better be spent in other ways. Rev Russell had to proceed with caution and distance himself from it personally, and it was not until a year later, in September 2003, that another member felt able to come back to the Meeting with revised proposals. The changes were then agreed, but not unanimously, and were implemented with the help of grants from the Property Board and the J Arthur Rank Trust. The cost was £17,300, with additional expenditure involved in the removal of the organ. The cross which now stands at the back of the sanctuary area was made out of wood from one of the redundant pews.

With hindsight most members would now agree that the changes were beneficial, as the church has greatly enjoyed the participation of children in Family Services. Bringing the choir and the organ down to ground level opened up the choir gallery for use by those leading the service and also made it possible to introduce a projection screen on which the words of hymns and announcements could be displayed, in line with contemporary practice. It was not an ideal arrangement, however, and in 2011 the Church Council resolved to spend £15,000 installing a new audio-visual system with superior LED screens each side of the sanctuary area, as the choir gallery was now called.

Robert Russell continued the practice of holding a Holiday Bible Club for Primary children in the school holidays, and although it has not taken place every year it has been held in most years, and always with great success.

In 2003 Robert Russell introduced the Alpha Course as the church's main outreach programme. The first Alpha course started in January 2003, and there were others in the Methodist Church and elsewhere in the town over the next couple of years. It was regarded by those who took part as extremely valuable, and Robert Russell encouraged all members of the Quarterly Meeting – and if possible all members of the congregation – to take part.

Towards the end of 2003 the church advertised for a part-time Youth and Family worker, but there was no response. The following year, however, a young woman, Pamela McCrea, was recruited, who fulfilled that role for three years. She produced the idea of the Sunday School as 'Workshop', 'shaping kids for eternity', as she put it. She was extremely popular with the children.

After a short interval she was replaced in 2008 by a young man, Jonny Nixon, who served for nearly two years before moving elsewhere. He did very good work, especially with the teenagers and those involved with sport of various kinds, but as with his predecessor it did not prove easy to integrate his work with the rest of the church's activities.

In 2011 the church advertised again for a part-time youth worker (omitting the reference to family work this time) but was unable to appoint. Nevertheless at the time of writing it is still a live issue: the church feels the need for an input into work with young people by someone who is nearer to them in age, but it is not easy to define the role exactly or to find the right person to fill it.

In 2004 the church building – but only the main church building – was listed by the Environment Agency. This greatly increased the difficulty of making any changes to the exterior and even to the interior, and is a constraint on any future plans for redevelopment.

Also in that year there were conversations with the churches in Glastry and Portaferry about the possibility of establishing a joint Circuit with them, but those conversations came to nothing.

That summer the Quarterly Meeting agreed that the church should start morning services at 11am, instead of 11.30, in June, July and August to facilitate visitors to the town. The change proved popular, and Morning Worship never reverted to the later time.

In 2005 the Methodist Church in Ireland published its 'Connexions' proposals, in light of which the Quarterly Board and Leaders' Meetings were replaced by a single, and much smaller, Church Council. This proposal was put to the Congregational Meeting in May 2005 and the Church Council was duly constituted.

In 2007 Rev Winston Graham came to the Circuit as a Retired Minister after 41 years in the active Ministry, most of it in circuit Ministry around Ireland, but also abroad. He served for nine years in the Overseas Division, and his last appointment was as

Secretary of the Methodist Church in Ireland. He was President of Conference in 2002-03. He has given great support to the church, especially during the Minister's absence on Sabbatical.

In early 2009 the Church Council, concerned about the steady drain of expenditure on maintaining the manse at 64 Millisle Road, resolved to sell it and purchase a more modern and more manageable property. They kept spending on repairs to a minimum and the property team began the search for a new manse. After considering several options they made an offer for, and purchased, 34 Breckenridge, which was therefore available for the new Minister, Rev Ruth Craig and her family to move in to in the late summer.

Selling the old manse proved more difficult in an adverse property market, but fortunately the bank made available a bridging loan on favourable terms and the 64 Millisle Road was sold in March 2010 for a sum which very nearly balanced the cost of the new manse. In all respects it was a highly successful operation, with the new manse offering much more satisfactory accommodation than the old.

Rev Ruth Craig and the present state of the church

Rev Ruth Craig succeeded Robert Russell in 2009 and is the Superintendent Minister at the time of writing. Born in 1962, she entered Edgehill College in 1994 and was appointed to Glenavy and other churches in the Moira area in 1997. She became a Minister in full connexion in 1999. Immediately prior to coming to Donaghadee she served as an Assistant Minister at Knock.

Donaghadee Methodist Church is still a warm, welcoming and viable congregation, with around 150 members on the Roll – up 15 per cent since the beginning of the millennium - and attendances of about 100 in the morning and 25 at evening Services. It has a choir, a Sunday School, a Girls' Brigade company and a strong MWI branch, as well as a Lunch Club catering for the older members and a Bowling Fellowship. It pays its way financially, and has some reserves invested against the day when there will need to be a major investment in the property, whether on the present site or on a new site – though redevelopment has been made more difficult by the fact that the church is now a listed building.

It is a church with a particular interest in overseas missions. Not only does it support missionary and humanitarian work financially, but several members are personally involved, one travelling regularly to Uganda, another going out to Haiti to help with relief work after the earthquake there, while another has family who are missionaries in Papua New Guinea and visits them there. That gives the church a special empathy with issues in poorer and hotter parts of the world.

The main concern would be that the congregation is becoming increasingly elderly, reflecting the fact that Donaghadee is seen as a desirable place for retirement. When one looks back at the church records over the past century, the overwhelming impression is one of stability and continuity. The same family names appear on the Church Council or the Quarterly Board, leading the Sunday School or running the youth activities, from one generation to another. The continuity is even more apparent if one looks at the maiden names of leading women in the congregation.

Other families have come in, but not many families with young children, and catering for the needs of post-primary children has proved a challenge. As people are living longer, the cultural gap between the generations has become wider than ever and it has become hard for older people, even with the best of intentions, to provide what the young are looking for. A church has to cater for the members it has, however, and it has to respect the fact that many are attached to the old building and the familiar ways of doing things.

The buildings have seen better days and will have to be replaced or extensively modernised before long. They are not well suited to the church's purposes nowadays, their appearance is old-fashioned and unappealing, and they are expensive to heat and maintain. But it is hard to see the money that would be needed for a wholesale redevelopment becoming available in current circumstances.

Catering for a Church Lunch, 2011

Then and now

On balance, those who founded the church back in 1813 would probably be pleased to see how well their institution has survived. They would recognise much of the church's worship, though they might be slightly shocked to hear an organ and to find Holy Communion being celebrated in a Methodist Chapel[144]. They would be surprised to find hymn books available for all, never mind the words appearing magically on screens at the front of the church.

---

[144] In 1813 Methodists would have gone to the Parish Church for Holy Communion, and for marriages and funerals.

They might be concerned by the relatively low attendance at Evening Worship, creditable though it is by today's standards, and by the small numbers in the Sunday School. They might miss the searching confessions that used to take place in Methodist Class Meetings and the personal testimonies that characterised the old Love Feasts.

But they would be pleased to see the warm fellowship of the church, its generosity, the pastoral care it extends, the weekly Bible classes which so many members attend – successors to their own Class Meetings – its commitment to the local community and the friendly relations the Methodist Church enjoys with all the other churches in the town: 'friends of all and enemies of none', as John Wesley used to say.

Jack Martin retired in 2011 at the age of 90, having been Church Caretaker for 21 years

Appendix 1

The Church Council and other officers, 2012-2013

The Rev Ruth Craig

Minister:	Rev Ruth Craig
Circuit Steward:	Joe Wright
Society Steward:	Geraldine Brown
Hon Treasurer:	Bill Parkinson
Council Secretary:	Cathryn McDade
Property Steward:	Dermot Thompson
Pastoral Convener:	Robert Watson
Council Members:	Brian Douglas
	Leonard Kirk
	Maeve Lennie
	Eleanor Halliday
	Maureen Bell
	Stephen Gibson

APPENDICES TO PART TWO

Other officers

Organist and Choirmaster:	Robert Watson
Sunday School Superintendent:	Hilda Butler
MWI President:	Winifred Thurley
Girls' Brigade Captain:	Elizabeth Brown
Friendship Club Convener:	Brian Douglas
Events Committee Convener:	Ken Halliday
Secretary of the Bowling Fellowship:	Fred Finch

Local Preachers

Robert Watson	Alan Craig
Maeve Lennie	Shirley Krakowski (on note)
Joan Parkinson	

Class Leaders

Norma Heaney	Joe Wright
Pat Caldwell	Jenny Watson
Vivienne Glasgow	Derek Clegg
Pearl Moffitt	Fiona Morrison
Maureen Bell	Kate Morphey
Hugh Herron	Marion Thompson
Margaret Connell	Eleanor Halliday
Eddie Davidson	Charlie Bell
David Gregory	Helen Johnston
Brian Douglas	Maureen Parks
Stanley Brown	Ann Holmes
Joan Bell	

Appendix 2

Ministers at Donaghadee
1913 – 2012

Note: 'Sup' stands for Supernumerary or Retired Minister

1913	Henry McConnell	
1915	Robert Maxwell	
1919	Robert J J Teasey	
1923	William McVitty	
1926	William E Maguire	
1928	William Bryans	
1930	Charles Wilson	
1934	F H Scott Maguire	
1939	Robert G McDonagh,	William McVitty
1943	Robert G McDonagh,	William McVitty (Sup)
1944	Samuel G McIntyre,	William McVitty (Sup)
1947	Samuel H Baxter MA,	William McVitty (Sup)
1952	Samuel J Crawford,	William McVitty (Sup)
1955	Thomas J Kyle,	William McVitty (Sup)
1956	Thomas J Kyle	
1959	Thomas J Kyle,	W E Morley Thompson (Sup)
1960	Robert J Good,	W E Morley Thompson (Sup)
1964	Robert J Good,	R Hull Spence (Sup), W E Morley Thompson (Sup)
1965	H L Frank Bolster,	W E Morley Thompson (Sup)
1969	H L Frank Bolster	
1972	H L Frank Bolster,	Samuel J Crawford

APPENDICES TO PART TWO

1973	W J Wesley Gray,	Samuel J Crawford
1974	W J Wesley Gray,	Samuel J Crawford, William Megahey
1975	W J Wesley Gray,	Samuel J Crawford
1976	W J Wesley Gray	
1978	W J Wesley Gray,	William Megahey (Sup)
1980	W J Wesley Gray	
1981	Wilfred Agnew BA	
1988	George J Campbell	
1991	George J Campbell,	Wilfred Agnew BA (Sup)
1993	David Houston,	Wilfred Agnew BA (Sup)
1994	J Brownlee Glenny MA BSc PhD,	Wilfred Agnew BA (Sup)
2001	Robert Russell,	Wilfred Agnew BA (Sup)
2009	Ruth Craig BTh, MA, MPhil,	Wilfred Agnew BA (Sup) W Winston Graham (Sup)

Rev Winston Graham

Appendix 3

Photographs of Church Organisations

The Church Council

Left to right: Stephen Gibson, Leonard Kirk, Robert Watson, Bill Parkinson *(Hon Treasurer)*, Geraldine Brown *(Society Steward)*, Rev Ruth Craig, Cathryn McDade *(Secretary)*, Joe Wright *(Circuit Steward)*, Dermot Thompson, Maeve Lennie, Brian Douglas

(photo: Rev Bert Montgomery)

APPENDICES TO PART TWO

The Choir: *(back row)* Jack Lennie, Brian Douglas, Charlie Bell; (middle row) Kate Morphey, Marion Thompson, Joyce Davidson, Rae Wright, Dorothy Mills; *(front row)* Margaret Breadon, Joan Bell, Winifred Thurley, Patsy Martin.   *Organist and Choirmaster:* Robert Watson   *(photo: Rev Bert Montgomery)*

Sunday School Teachers: Blanche Graham, Geraldine Brown, Margaret Taylor, Hilda Butler *(Superintendent)*, Eleanor Halliday

APPENDICES TO PART TWO

The Girls' Brigade, Captain: Elizabeth Brown

MWI Committee: (left to right) Loy Brown, Patsy Martin, Maureen Parks, Helen Johnston, Joan Brown, (front) Valerie Hanna, Winifred Thurley, Jennifer Watson

Annual Dinner of the Bowling Fellowship

Postscript

Winston Churchill is one of the two people credited with having said, "History is just one darned thing after another"[145]. The reader might conclude that that is true of this book. It often seems that one thing just happens after another. History is not like a novel. There is no plot, and indeed no ending.

And yet, to Jews and Christians alike – indeed to all the peoples of the Book – history is more than that. Their history was their identity, and it was what the German professors call 'Heilsgeschichte', salvation history. It showed the developing interaction of a people with a God who was their Saviour.

That is why history was a priority for the Jews of the Old Testament. Every child was taught by heart the history of Abraham, "A wandering Aramaean was my father..", and the story of the Passover, which was and still is celebrated in each Jewish family every year.

As individuals, we are no more than our memories. Our memories are what connect us as we are today to the people we were when we were younger. There is no atom in my body that is the same as when I was 21. Physically I am no relation to my former self: my memories are the only things that constitute my identity. When a person loses his memory we sometimes say, "It's not him any more".

---

[145] The other is Arnold Toynbee. They actually said, "One damn thing after another", but that would not be proper in a church history.

That is true of a church and of a nation, too. Our identity as Donaghadee Methodist Church consists of our common memories and traditions. So our history matters. But it is a double-edged sword.

The remembrance of time past can lead to nostalgia. Just as we would all (perhaps) like to be 21 again, so the church (or many of us in the church) would like to be back in the 1950s, which may now seem like glory days by comparison with the present.

But what history teaches us, if we look at it over the long haul, is that there has to be change. The present is not like the past, and it never will be.

The history of Judaism and Christianity is a story of progressively letting go of things. First, we let go of human sacrifice (Abraham and Isaac), then of animal sacrifice. We let go of ritual, ceremonies and priestcraft. We let go of circumcision and dietary rules. We no longer think sick people or women who have just given birth are 'unclean'. We have let go of national and racial prejudices and gender discrimination – or at least, we are getting there!

Letting go is always painful, but there is more to be done. A sense of history should give us the confidence to go forward into the future knowing that it will not be like the past and cannot be, but that God will be with us, and it will be good.

Bibliography

Allen, Harry, *Donaghadee, an illustrated history* (2006) The White Row Press

Anon, *A Candid and Impartial Inquiry into the Present State of the Methodist Societies in Ireland* (1814) J Commins, Lincoln's Inn

Averell, Adam, *The Memoirs of Mrs Dorothea Johnson* (1818) J O'Brien

Brewer, J D, **Higgins,** G I and **Teeney,** F, *Religion, Civil Society and Peace in Northern Ireland* (2011) Oxford Press

Cole, R L, *History of Methodism in Ireland 1860-1960* (1960) Epworth House, Belfast

Cooney, Dudley L, *The Methodists in Ireland* (2001) Columba Press, Dublin

Crookshank, Charles H, *History of Methodism in Ireland* (1885) R S Allen and Son, Belfast

Crookshank, Charles H, *Memorable Women of Irish Methodism in the last Century* (1882) Wesleyan Methodist Book Room, London

Curnock, Nehemiah (Ed) *Journals of John Wesley* (1909) R Culley, London

Gallagher, Eric, *At Points of Need* (1990), The Blackstaff Press

Haire, Robert, *The Story of the '59 Revival,* undated and published privately, printed by Nelson and Knox Ltd.

Haire, Robert, *Wesley's One and Twenty Visits to Ireland* (1947) The Epworth Press, London

Hattersley, Roy, *A Brand from the Burning* (2002) Little, Brown

Hill, John, *Memoir of Mrs and Miss Smith* (1858) Sentinel Press, Londonderry

Jackson, Alvin, *Home Rule: an Irish history 1800-2000* (2003) Weidenfeld and Nicholson

Kyle, Thomas, *History of Donaghadee Methodist Church* (1959)

published privately by the church

Lanktree, Matthew, *Biographical Narrative* (1836) James Wilson, Belfast

MacGowan, John, *Reminiscences* (1884) published privately

Stewart, Alexander and **Revington**, George, *Memoir of the Life and Labours of the Rev Adam Averell* (1848) Methodist Book Room, Dublin

Index

Adams, Miss J 143,154,156
Agnew, Rev Wilfred 173
Aldrey, Alan 40
Alpha Course 193
America, Americans 19,21,70
Anglican, Anglicans: see Church of Ireland
Ardill family 142
Ardmillan 58
Ards 20,27,65,69,99,101
 - Mission 28,58,96,98
Averell, Rev Adam 23,40,45
Back Street 13,76
Ballard, Rev Thomas 62,103
Ballyblack 77,98
Ballygrainey 13,73
Band of Hope 73
Bangor 13,24,60,65,66,88,110,125
Baptismal Roll 40,59,67,101-104
Baptist Chapel 172
Barnsley, Mrs 42,67
Barracks, Donaghadee 22,33,46,63
Baxter, Rev Samuel 139-143
Belfast 12,15,16,19,27-29,61,65,74, 81,84,88,89,96,102,134
Belfast City Mission 70,127-129,143
Bell, Charles and Maureen 5,109
 - Joan 188,189
Bird, Elizabeth 5
Bolster, Rev Frank 151,160-164
Borstal 174
Bowen, Robert 175
Bowling Fellowship 150,196
Boys' Brigade 155, 162

Britain, British Government 18-24, 64,112
Broadbelt, Rev John 142
Brown, Rev Wm 69
Bryans, Rev William 125
Burrows, Rev Michael 62
Butler, Hilda 186
Calvinism 54-57
Campbell family 141,153,158
Campbell, Rev George 176-179
Carey, Antony 37,46
Carey, Mary 11,12,28-33,47,63
Carrowdore 40,77
Cather, Rev William 67
Catholics, Catholic Church 18,20,23-25,58,59,64,79,166,167
Chatterbox 188
Childhaven 127-129,149,185
Children's Church 146,172,191
Cholera 14,63,96,100
Christian Endeavour 130,140,141, 148, 150,152,162,163,166,172
Church buildings (Donaghadee Methodist):
 - *1813*: 12,33,37-42,49
 - *1849*: 50,68.77,83,84
 - *1909*: 85-88,110,177
Church Council 192,194,196,200
Church of Ireland 18,20,25,36,40, 50-55,172,191
Church Parlour 136,138,148
Circuits 27,28,61,72,96,99, 100,155,176,194
Clarke, Dr Adam 62

213

Class meetings 53,77
Cliff College 135,142,160
Coke, Rev Dr 19
Coleraine 21,96
Comber 28,96,126
Communion, Holy 50,52,53,73, 76,122,198
Conference, Methodist 17,27,39,40, 51-53,56,60,61,83,99,154,166,167
'Connect' Christian Counselling 188, 190
Copeland Islands 14,70,96-98,150
Corn-kiln 12,29,30
Cottown 98
Cownley, Joseph 27
Craig, Rev Ruth 195
Crawford, Rev Samuel 146-151
Dalzell, Andrew and Thomas 40,103
Davidson, Edward 158, James 38?
Delacherois, Daniel 12,24,41,51
Delacherois family 16,43,44
Derriaghy 33-36
Donaghadee Male Voice Choir 133, 136
Donaghadee Resolutions 19
Doolittle, Rev Thomas 41
Doran, Wilson 181
Douglas, Margaret 189
Drop-in Centre 181
Dublin 14-18,24-27,45,56
Edwards, John 27
Emberson, Robert 97-99
– (Jr) 117
'Epworth' see Manses
Famine 24,64,65,79
Fergie, William 5,109
Ferguson, John 73
Fire of 1976 170-173
First Presbyterian Church 17,66
France, French 19-22

Funerals 72,191
Gallagher, Rev Dr Eric 129,162,167
Gayer, Mrs Henrietta 33-36,46,49
- William and Edward 34,35
- Mary (Mrs Wolfenden) 35,36
Gibson, Rev T E 125
Girls' Brigade 147,162,172,196
Girls' League 131,141,156
Glastry 142,175,194
Glenny, Rev Brownlee 183-186
Good, Rev Robert 157-158
Gordon, John 77
Grace, Rev 27
Graham, Rev Winston 191, 194-195, 203
Gransha 77, 102
Gray, Rev Wesley 168-170
Greer, Rev John 71
Grey Abbey 58
Halliday, Kenneth 5
Harpur, Rev Samuel 62,63,96
Hermon, Lady Sylvia 189
Herron, Hugh 109
High Street 13,29
- Presbyterian, see First Presbyterian Church
Hill, Rev John 16,46,47,49,68,93,98, 117
Home Missions 76,88,121,135,136
Home Rule 79-80,92,112,113
Houston, Rev David 182
Howe, Rev 27
Hull, Major and Mrs 42,59
- Rev Thomas T N 44,59,60,78
- Robert 82
Huntingdon, Countess of 56
Jamison, Rev Robert 76,81
Johnson, Dorothea 45-49,95
– Rev John 46
Johnston, Charles H 82

214

INDEX

- Rev Crawford 81,128
Junior Church, see Children's Church
Keys, Rev William 62
Killaughey (Killaghy) 40,58,134
Killaughey Road 110
Knox, Rev and Hon Charles 53
Kyle, Rev Thomas 28,150,152-157
Lanktree, Rev Dr Matthew 15,21, 28,37,51,52,57,58,63,96-100
Lee, Albert 158
Lennie, Maeve 189
Lisburn 33,34,41-46,49,52,88
London 14,15
Love feasts 29,75
Loyalism, Loyalists 20,23
Lunch Club 196
McConnell, Rev Henry 113
- William 38,40
McCracken, Mrs 42
McCutcheon, Jane 31,63
McDonagh, Rev Robert 133,134
MacGowan, John 43,77,85
McIntyre, Rev Samuel 137-139
McMillan, Arthur 82,90,91,115
MacMinn, Mrs 42,43
McVitty, Rev William 123,124,139
Maguire, Rev Francis Scott 129
- Rev William E 125
Manor Street 13,76
Manse, Donaghadee Methodist:
-*1822*, 'The Old Manse' 33,39,61,68, 81,86
-*1836*, 'Wesley Lodge' 63,68,81
-*1893*, 'Epworth' 63,81,137, 153,163
-*1969*, 'Epworth' 164,194,195
-*2009*, Breckenridge 195
Marriage 50,71
Maxwell, Rev Robert 117
Mayes, Alexander 82
Mayne, Rev Charles 41,46,47

Methodist College 71,166
Methodist Newsletter 166
Methodist Women in Ireland 196
Methodist Women's Association 156
Millisle Road 13,33,63,66,110
Mills, Brian and Dorothy 5,109
Moat St (or Mound St) 13,42
- No. 8 Moat St 176,179,180,184, 185
Mork, Thomas 77
Morrison, Rev R M 80
- William 77,81
Music 74,150,186
Napoleonic Wars 17,43
New Street 13,66
Newry 15,27,28
Newtownards 12,22,26,28,60,61,72, 96,99,102,121
Nixon, Jonny 193
North Down 27,176
Norwell, Mrs 42
Old Choir Room, see Church Parlour
Old Manse, see Manses
Orange Order 20
Organ 74,121-123,141-143,192
– blower 121,135
Organist 142,143,154,162
Orphans' Fund 76,82,90
- Society 126
Ouseley, Rev Gideon 59
Pacification, Plan of 51,52
Penal Laws 18,64
Pew rents 122
Phillips, Rev Randall 21,23
Poor Fund 75
Portaferry 22,58,194
Portavo 42,98
Portpatrick 14,15,26,65
Presbyterian, - Church 19,20,52, 54-57,69

Primitive Wesleyan Church 41,52,53
Quarry Green 122,141,150,151,157
Quarterly Meeting 114,117,121,141, 155,179,185,193
Railway 13,66,110
Rank Benevolent Trust 171, 192
Reeves, Rt Rev William 36
Revival 69
Robertson, Mrs 77
Roddie, Rev Wesley 114
Russell, Rev Robert 187-192
Salvation Army 150
Sankey and Moody 74,75
Schoolhouse Brae 66
School:
- Admiral Leslie 172
- Church Day 50,67,68,70,73,82, 115-117,127,131,144,147
- Donaghadee Primary 147,172
- Mount Alexander 43
- National 66
- Sunday 11,30,39,40,69,70,77,82, 90,115,116,122,191,193,196
Semphill, Mrs Marianne 42,43
Sexton 121,147
Shore Street 13
- Presbyterian Church 17,172
Skillen, Rev Hamilton 165
Smith, Anne 32,37,44,47,48,67
Smith, Mary 12,25,31-33,37,39,41, 43,46-50,63,67,68,78,93-95
Smyth, Rev James 89
Steele, Rev Samuel 33,37,38,54
Stone, Mrs 141,178
Sturgeon, Rev Alexander 62
Swindells, Robert 27
Sunday School, see School
Teacher's residence 67,82,87,147, 153
Teasey, Rev Robert 120-122

Temperance 72,73
Tennis Club 140,150
Thompson, Dermot 26
Tone, Wolfe 19-23
Ulster 27,28,65,79,112
United Irishmen 19-22,46
Wales, Welsh 56
Wallace, Martin 115
Warren Road 13,66,110,111
Watson, Mr Robert 162
Waugh, Rev David 60,96
Wedgewood, Rev George 84
Wesley, Rev Charles 55,75
- Rev John 21,26,27,34-36,46, 50,55,72,81
Wesley Hall 147,176,184
'Wesley Lodge', see Manses
Whitley, Dr 102
Whittington, Ernest 174
Wilkinson, Arthur 131,147
Wilson, Rev Charles 126
Wisheart, Rev James 145
Wolfenden, Mary see Gayer, Mary
Women's Department 156,163
Wood, Rev Samuel 46
Wright, Dorothy 162
Youth and Family Worker 181,193
Youth for Christ 180,186

THE AUTHOR

Kit Chivers was Church Council Secretary 2009 - 2012. He was Secretary of the Student Christian Movement at Oxford, and for 20 years Secretary of the Brixton Council of Churches, in which capacity he wrote for the *Guardian* on theology and religious affairs. A member of the Equality Commission and the Consumer Council, he was made CBE in 2009 for services to justice in Northern Ireland.